THE NEW AGE
OF
FRANKLIN ROOSEVELT
1932–45

The New Age of

THE CHICAGO HISTORY OF AMERICAN CIVILIZATION

Daniel J. Boorstin, EDITOR

Franklin Roosevelt, 1932-45

By Dexter Perkins

 THE UNIVERSITY OF CHICAGO PRESS
CHICAGO AND LONDON

Library of Congress Catalog Card Number: 56-11263

THE UNIVERSITY OF CHICAGO PRESS, CHICAGO & LONDON
The University of Toronto Press, Toronto 5, Canada

© *1957 by The University of Chicago. Published 1957. Eighth
Impression 1964. Composed and printed by* THE UNIVERSITY
OF CHICAGO PRESS, *Chicago, Illinois, U.S.A.*

Editor's Preface

Those critical periods when leaders emerge, issues are sharpened, and new institutions take shape, by an unhappy human necessity tend to leave us the most biased story of themselves. All historians would agree that the age of Franklin Roosevelt (1932–45) was just such a period and that it has left us very few accounts which are neither defenses nor indictments. Interpreting that age is all the more difficult because it lies now only partly below the horizon of personal recollection: for about half the readers of this volume it remains a vivid memory; for the rest it is almost as unlived as the American Revolution or the Civil War.

While Professor Dexter Perkins himself possesses the advantage of personal memory of many of the events recounted, he has succeeded in giving us a fair-minded and good-tempered interpretation. Most important, he has managed to raise his story above personality into the broad perspective of history. This story shows us many vigorous actors, but not a cast of heroes and villains. The form and drama of that era, according to Professor Perkins, lie in the large changes which made it a grand epoch in American history, not in the fact that either New Dealers or their enemies were the

Editor's Preface

exclusive champions of pure American values. He sees American values emergent from our developing institutions, a response to the needs of a compromising, adaptable, decent, and hopeful people. The novel institutions, so he tells us, came not from the vision of one man or one party but as the complex result of the pragmatism, imagination, and passions of F. D. R. and his followers, inhibited and deflected by the firmly held principles and interests of those who opposed him and hedged about by the indifference of many more—all on an American landscape with its own peculiar features.

No partisan will be wholly satisfied by this account, but everyone can learn from it how partisan issues become transformed in the eye of the historian. Professor Perkins helps us see how the conflicts of the age came to be framed in a characteristically American manner. His story is concise and simple, offering an inviting bridge from the general reader to the professional historian.

Such is the broad purpose of the "Chicago History of American Civilization," which aims to enliven the historical literature, to invigorate it with judgments, and to enrich it with the best and most recent scholarship. The series contains two general classes of volumes: a *chronological* group, which will provide a coherent narrative of American history from its beginning to the present day, and a *topical* group, which will deal in turn with the history of varied and important aspects of American life. This book is one of the chronological group. Twenty-odd volumes are in preparation; those already published are listed at the end of this volume.

DANIEL J. BOORSTIN

Preface

The title of this book suggests its theme. It attempts to trace, in brief form, the momentous economic, political, and foreign-policy changes in the United States during the Roosevelt administrations. Telling the full story would require many volumes. All that I have tried to do here is to offer some insights into the times and into the nature of the President with whom the times are indelibly associated.

The book has been read by a variety of specialists, by Arthur M. Schlesinger, Jr., by John Kenneth Galbraith, both of Harvard University, and by two of my colleagues at Cornell University, Alfred Kahn and Paul W. Gates. I have profited greatly from their criticisms. I am grateful also to Daniel J. Boorstin, editor of this series, for his constructive suggestions. My assistants at Cornell, David A. Tiffany and Lin Webster, have ably performed some special tasks in connection with this work. Finally, for the seventh time, I acknowledge the services of my secretary, Miss Marjorie Gilles. I find no new words with which to express the appreciation that I feel and have made manifest in previous prefaces so far as she is concerned.

Table of Contents

Prologue

Why is this book called "the new age of Roosevelt"? The phrase ought not to carry with it any suggestion that the problems of American society were solved between 1932 and 1945. History offers no such promise of finality to its votaries. It provides, rather, an unending series of renascent hopes and recurrent fears. Each generation has its own interpretation of what came before; and the age of Roosevelt will mean, to the student of 2056, something very different from what it means to the student today. The new age will then have become an old one.

Nor does the phrase "the new age of Roosevelt" suggest a total contrast between 1932–45 and the years that preceded. At the end of the period the free political institutions in which the American people had always taken pride were as strong as—and perhaps stronger than—ever before; the economic organization of the country was still based upon capitalism, as distinguished from socialism, as all of us can see today; the social stirrings expressed in the New Deal—distrust of the concentration of wealth, the strong desire to ameliorate the lot of the less fortunate—none of these was absent from the history that had gone before. Nor was it a new thing for the people of the United States to find themselves

1

involved in a world war in which their idealism and their interests were both engaged. No chronological division ever does justice to the facts of history. No "age" stands by itself.

Yet the new age of Roosevelt *was* new, and it behooves us at the beginning of this survey to understand why it was new. It was new because, in the first place, it emphasized, as never before, the dynamic role of the federal government. The reformist zeal of earlier periods as, for example, of the Progressive era, analyzed by Professor Hofstadter with such illumination, had emphasized the regulatory role of the state. The Roosevelt years extended this role. But they introduced something else. They introduced a positive conception of responsibility never emphasized before, responsibility, it will be seen, to relieve want and unemployment through the federal agencies, responsibility for providing for the farmer a larger part of the national product, responsibility for the development of national resources on a more grandiose scale, responsibility for the maintenance of industrial peace, enlarged responsibility for the operation of the nation's credit system. Nor was this all. The economic orthodoxies of an earlier period were severely shaken by the New Deal. In previous depressions it had been supposed that the thing to do was to cut expenses and balance the budget. In the Roosevelt years, though not precisely through design or clear acceptance of another view, the unbalancing of the budget in difficult times became not only current practice but defensible in theory. One has only to read today the literature of the business-minded Committee for Economic Development to see how far we have moved since 1933.

We may go further. The Roosevelt era represented substantial alterations in the economic order. The balance of power between the most important groups was substantially changed. Unionism, especially industrial unionism, attained a much greater importance.

Prologue

The farmer, neglected in the twenties, attained a new political power. The less fortunate economic groups became more self-conscious than ever before and more disposed to exert their influence. And, paradoxically enough, along with all this went an immense increase, in the second half of the period, in the scope and sweep of American business enterprise, in the magnitude of the tasks performed by the industrial machine, in technological advance. Never before, as the epoch closed, had men faced a future so brightly illuminated with the hope of scientific progress and widening productivity.

The change was no less real in the field of foreign affairs. American participation in World War I was a small affair compared with participation in World War II. The year 1920 had seen a real reaction away from involvement in world affairs. The years after 1945 saw new complications, new commitments, new interpretations of the American role. Though the flowing tide may ebb again, though a new mood of withdrawal may conceivably throw the American people back upon themselves, the old provincialism has been severely shaken, if not destroyed. Nor was this all. No one could doubt the portentous significance of the bombs that fell on Hiroshima and Nagasaki. The experiments in nuclear power, begun with so much audacity and so much vision by the Roosevelt administration, could not fail to alter profoundly the thinking of a new generation. They were, most emphatically, the portents of a new age.

These generalizations, however, must not deceive us. The story of the Roosevelt years in domestic affairs is a story of adjustment, not of revolution. The story of American foreign policy in these same years is the story of acceptance of a role long foreshadowed, if reluctantly undertaken. Let us soberly examine the facts, the concrete developments, of the years 1933–45.

3

I

The Two Phases of the Early New Deal

The year 1932 was one of the gloomiest in the history of the republic. Millions of industrial workers out of a job tramped the streets of our cities, and in New York unemployed men were trying to earn a miserable living by selling apples on Fifth Avenue. Bread lines were forming in the poorer districts, and hundreds of indigent people waited patiently for a pitiful handout of food; whole families of people, evicted from their homes, were sleeping in rudely constructed shacks or even in doorways and on the ground. Farmers were blocking highways and stopping milk trucks in protest against the fall in the price of their product, or they were resisting the authority of the sheriff, come to drive them from their homes. On the Anacostia flats in Washington were encamped the so-called bonus marchers, come to Washington to seek aid from their government, until evicted by federal troops commanded by General MacArthur in full uniform. Brokers and bankers trembled at what the future might bring; and a tired President struggled desperately to redress the balance of a distressed country. Men talked of revolution, and intelligent people, including some of

4

the leading lights in the field of American literature, indorsed a Communist candidate for President of the United States.

And yet the mass of the American people did not give way to despair or seek the path of violent change. When election day came in November, they trooped to the polls in large numbers, but they did not express themselves in any radical way. They merely turned from one of the two traditional parties to the other. The Communists, with more favorable conditions than they were ever to meet again, could poll only 120,000 votes in more than 45 million. The Socialists could reach only 887,000, proportionately far less than they had won in 1920, or even back in 1912. With a moderation that was matched in most of the great democracies of Europe (though not in hard-pressed Germany), by the use of the normal machinery of popular government and in remarkably good order, they elected a Democratic President of the United States.

It cannot be said that the people who voted for Franklin Roosevelt in 1932 could be very sure of what they were getting. They could know quite a little about the candidate. They could know that he had been a vigorous and successful Assistant Secretary of the Navy in the Wilson administration and the unsuccessful Democratic candidate for Vice-President in 1920. They could know that shortly after this election he had been stricken with infantile paralysis and had, with heroic resolve, fought his way back to active life. They could know that he had been elected governor of New York in 1928 by a narrow margin and had been overwhelmingly re-elected in 1930 by a plurality of approximately 700,000. They could find in his administration as governor evidences of capacity in his successful advocacy of measures for assistance to agriculture and evidences of his social sympathy in his solicitude for the unemployed and in his vigorous handling of the problem of relief. Their enthusiasm might have been tempered by his far from militant attitude in dealing with the corruption in New York City characteristic of Tammany Hall at its worst.

But, whatever their knowledge, they were hardly voting for a coherent program. The Democratic candidate in the course of his campaign *did* mention at one time or another many of the ideas that were later to be translated into action, and in a famous speech at the Commonwealth Club at San Francisco he came nearest to putting them together to form a whole. Nevertheless, it can hardly be said that he deviated from the standard campaign practice of attempting to please as many groups as possible. His enemies were later to recall his promises to balance the budget, his emphasis on a sound currency, and his remarkable evasions on the subject of the protective tariff. The idea of a mature economy (one that had reached its limit of expansion), which was implicit in some of his utterances, stands today in diametrical opposition to the experience of our own time. Walter Lippmann's often quoted and depreciatory comment that Roosevelt was a "pleasant man who, without any important qualifications for the office, would like very much to be President," although extreme, did not seem altogether absurd to the critical in 1932.

Time was to prove it wide of the mark. Few Presidents of the United States have aroused a deeper contemporaneous devotion, and none, by the political law of action and reaction, has provoked a deeper detestation. No other American political leader has appeared to so many Americans as the good or evil genius of his epoch. From the day when he appeared on the east porch of the Capitol to proclaim to the American people that they had "nothing to fear but fear itself" to the day when he was fatally stricken at Warm Springs, he was the central figure of the American scene.

He not only presided over an era of social change but also held the confidence of the American people through the most serious international crisis that the country had ever faced; and after more than twelve years in the Presidency he died a world figure in a sense that had never been true of any other Chief Executive (save possibly Woodrow Wilson in the days of his glory).

Why was Roosevelt so loved? Why was he so hated? On the positive account, the chief factor seemingly was his optimism and his sympathy with the less fortunate. Under Herbert Hoover the country had been submerged in gloom; the new President set a different tone from the very beginning. He believed that the difficulties he faced could be overcome; and his confidence in the future, at a time when so many people were miserable, was a tonic to a large part of the American people. He viewed the social suffering of the years of the Depression in terms of the hungry, the unemployed, the dispossessed, the underprivileged; and he made these groups feel that he cared. Again and again from such people there came the tribute, "He was thinking of us." It is true that this feeling for the "forgotten man" redounded to his political advantage, but no one could justly say that he merely sought votes for votes' sake. The program that he sponsored and put into effect was the refutation of any such cynical assumption; he did not betray those for whom and to whom he appealed.

The matter can be stated in another way. Roosevelt believed that American society could be improved. His attitude toward politics was dynamic, not static. At a time when the American people were hungry for action, he gave them action; and in the perspective that we have today, he left behind a social fabric stronger than that which existed in 1933.

But why was he hated as well as loved? Fundamentally, he seemed to his enemies to be shaking the foundations of the order which they had known and in which they had flourished. It is, of course, true that his administration represented a shift in the economic balance of power, a diminution in the influence of the business classes, and an enhancement of the role of the farmer and, still more important, the role of labor. No class willingly surrenders power, and large elements in the business class felt with reason that this was precisely what was being demanded of them. Moreover, Roosevelt shocked the orthodox by his jaunty attitude toward financial matters. He favored heavy taxes on the well-to-do, and he deemed a balanced budget less significant than the relief of the unemployed. To the orthodox both of these policies were highly distasteful. But there was more to the matter than that. The President's critics could point with some justice to the deviousness and indirection that was often a part of his political technique; they found his liking for experimentation, sometimes injudicious experimentation, extremely annoying; and they accused him, not wholly unjustly, of appealing to class antagonisms. It was a former president of the United States Chamber of Commerce who said sometime after Roosevelt's death that he had detested only one man in his life, and that that man lay buried in Hyde Park. The transcendent success of the President over a period of t\ .ve years naturally intensified the feeling typified by this remark.

How did Roosevelt succeed so well? He had certain personal gifts that were important. His radio addresses, his "fireside chats," a feature of his administration, were delivered in a warm and vibrant voice that breathed confidence in the future and arrested and held the attention of his listeners. His press conferences were masterpieces of technique, blending humor and seriousness, frankness and evasion, the significant and the trivial, in a way which won the hearts of most of the newsmen. In his dealings with people he could be extremely charming. In his capacity to evoke loyalty from his subordinates he was outstanding. Rifts there were, it is true, in the long period of his ascendancy, but the variety of the men whom he won to himself is astounding.

More than this, Roosevelt was a superb technician. His enemies called him a dictator. The charge will not stick. In general, no one was more sensitive to the public mood, more ready to translate it into action, more willing to be guided by it. The line between leading and following is sometimes a thin one. A successful politician does not develop his policies out of thin air. He catches the drift of opinion; he seeks to anticipate the inevitable; he sometimes allows his hand to be forced and sometimes speaks out boldly. He understands and uses the personal ambitions, antagonisms, and aspirations of those with whom he must work; he gives a little here and gains a little there. All these things were true of F. D. R. He knew that he was the leader of a democracy; he knew that he had to act with the concurrence of Congress to accomplish results; he knew that he had to reconcile conflicting wills and conflicting interests in the evolution of policy. That he did this successfully is attested by his re-election in 1936, 1940, and 1944.

This is not to say that Roosevelt did not enjoy power and exercise it. Especially in the field of foreign affairs, where a wide degree of personal authority is possible, the President, like his great namesake Theodore, often went far and sometimes strained the limits of constitutional authority. But even here, as we shall see later, the broad lines of policy were shaped by him in conjunction with the national legislature and were intelligently, sometimes subtly and often frankly, co-ordinated with public opinion.

The charge of autocracy leveled against him, we repeat, must be rejected. What gave it plausibility to his contemporaries, or at any rate to the more conservative among them, was that F. D. R. believed in a powerful national government operating in a wide field for the public weal. The position he took involves one of the great issues of American political history. American Chief Executives have been of two types: those who conceived of the office chiefly in terms of administration and of the federal mechanism as limited in scope, and those who believed that with the growth of the nation, and with the increasing complexity of its problems, more and more activities must be concentrated in Washington. The contrast between these two points of view is well illustrated by the difference between President Hoover and President Roosevelt. It is unfair to charge, as many of his critics have charged, that Hoover did nothing to check the Depression or to deal positively with the problems that it raised. But it is true that, running through the whole term of this most unhappy and unfortunate President, there was in his attitude toward his problems a profound distrust of governmental power. Occasionally this distrust was overcome, but for the most part reluctance to stretch the zone of federal authority was characteristic of the Hoover administration. It was far otherwise, as we shall see, with Franklin Roosevelt.

There is truth in both the Hoover and the Roosevelt view. There is such a thing as governmental gigantism; there is such a thing as a government that falls by its own weight. But there is also such a thing as governmental paralysis if too much stress is laid on federal inaction or on too far-reaching scruples as to the limits of federal authority; and, if we view the question in the perspective of the historian, we shall be bound to conclude that in the long run the Roosevelt view has been sustained by time. Government today, even though there has been a mild reaction from the period of the New Deal, exercises a wider power over the affairs of the nation.

To return to Roosevelt's techniques of government, even his

friendly critics have often said that the President was not a great administrator. He was no stickler for exact lines of authority; he viewed with complacency quarrels in his official family; he hated to dismiss officials who were incompetent or who had ceased to represent him; he sometimes bypassed his own cabinet officers, especially Cordell Hull, his long-suffering Secretary of State. But there is another side to the matter. He was a highly imaginative director of affairs: by setting goals that sometimes seemed fantastic, he often achieved results that a more cautious, run-of-the-mine Chief Executive could never have attained; and when his methods are laid beside the administrative accomplishments, the results seem impressive—particularly in the period of the war.

In addition, he brought to Washington a large number of competent and imaginative people from varying walks of life. The capital seethed with ideas, too many ideas for the cautious and conservative. Anything but a scholar by temperament, Roosevelt respected scholarship, and few administrations have been more active in recruiting those with special knowledge. Not a few of these people were professors; some were lawyers; some were businessmen. Harry Hopkins, of whom more anon, was a social worker. There has rarely been a more varied representation of points of view at Washington than in the New Deal administration.

But let us turn from the President himself to the story of the New Deal. In the long perspective, as already suggested, one of the most striking facts about the Roosevelt policies is the resentment they aroused among the business classes, not only among the masters of capital but frequently among the smaller entrepreneurs. But we shall misunderstand the whole problem if we assume that the President began in a proscriptive spirit. On the contrary, when he took office, he was thinking in terms of a great national effort toward recovery. He did not even wish this effort to be partisan. As late as March, 1934, he wrote to Colonel House: "My best judgment is that I should take part in no Jefferson Day dinner this year. Our strongest plea to the country in this particular year of grace is that the recovery and reconstruction program is being accomplished by men and women of all parties—that I have repeatedly appealed to Republicans as well as Democrats to do their part." And in the same spirit he sought at the outset to bring all economic groups, including the business group, into his program. During the first two years, the New Deal measures were, in many cases, in the interest of this group. There were also many measures that met with business opposition. Perhaps the best way to understand what actually occurred is to balance one against the other the policies which were on the whole acceptable to large elements of the capitalists and those which they disliked.

Let us look first at what became known as the "Hundred Days," that extraordinary period of legislative and executive activity with which the administration began. The Roosevelt handling of the banking crisis and the banking legislation which followed, the attempt to balance the budget, the measures taken for the relief of farm and home indebtedness, the relaxation of the restrictions on the sale of alcohol, represent one side of the account. All met with approval from many of those who later were to find the Roosevelt policies obnoxious.

The most universally praised of the President's actions was his dealing with the financial crisis. There had been a slight business upturn in the fall of 1932, but then demoralization set in. The banking system of the country was put under heavy pressure. There were already moratoriums in some of the most important states before Hoover left office. In February, 1933, the governor of Michigan proclaimed an eight-day bank holiday to check withdrawals. His example was followed in other states, and, when Roosevelt took office, the whole banking system was paralyzed. On Inauguration Day it was difficult to cash a check in Washington, and a situation of virtual collapse prevailed.

Roosevelt met this first emergency of his administration with vigor. He proclaimed a bank holiday throughout the country; he called Congress in special session to ratify his action; and he placed the banks of the nation under license. In the course of the weeks that followed, solvent banks were reopened as speedily as possible; over two thousand were compelled to wind up their affairs; and the confidence of the country in its banking system was re-established. That enormous losses were prevented by the strong action of the government can hardly be denied; from one to two billion hoarded dollars flowed back into the financial system of the nation.

Moreover, for years after 1933 the number of bank failures was reduced to a minimum. The annual average for the years down to 1940 was only forty-five, and the number of reserve-system members that failed was only three. The crisis of March led to legislation designed to prevent the abuses and perils of the past, and a banking act (Glass-Steagall Act) passed the Congress by impressive majorities, by 191 to 6 in the House on a final roll call and by a voice vote in the Senate. Under its terms a variety of important reforms was instituted. A system of federal guarantee of deposits was set up for all banks within the Federal Reserve System; commercial and investment banking (the source of many of the embarrass-ments of the previous era) were divorced; and the Federal Reserve System itself was reorganized to give to the governors of the Federal Reserve Board somewhat more control over the credit system of the country. This legislation was to be supplemented and strengthened by another banking act passed in 1935.

The New Age of Franklin Roosevelt, 1932–45

Even more striking and gratifying to the orthodox was the courageous action of the President in pressing an economy bill through the Congress. This measure cut government expenses drastically; and even the Veterans Bureau, the sacred cow of politically minded congressmen, was hard hit. Had the act been adhered to, the total savings might have been about $750 million, and the savings in payment to veterans alone were estimated at the astounding figure of $300 million.

A third achievement had to do with the relief of debtors. The Hoover regime had established Home Loan Banks; the New Deal set up the Home Owners Loan Corporation on a somewhat broader basis. The interests of both mortgagor and mortgagee were served by this device, and in the course of the next three years about a sixth of the urban home indebtedness in the United States was refinanced. In the same way, various agricultural credit agencies were consolidated into a single Farm Credit Administration that sought to do for farmers what the Home Owners Loan Corporation did for city-dwellers.

If we identify conservatism with distrust of the power of government, as we well may, there is another measure of the early period of the New Deal to be added to those we have mentioned. The Eighteenth Amendment to the Constitution of the United States, banning the manufacture and sale of alcohol, had been adopted in 1919. The "experiment noble in purpose," as President Hoover described it, had hardly vindicated itself in action. Prohibition may have been the most well intentioned of reforms, but the evidence suggests that it was very far from a success. It did not check—in fact it seems to have increased—the actual consumption of alcohol. It created a virtually insoluble problem of enforcement, and it gave rise to corruption and violence on a scale that could hardly have been foreseen and that was the more

14

appalling because it had not been anticipated. The Democratic convention of 1932 had called for the repeal of the amendment. Congress, after the decisive victory of the President, had sent the necessary repeal amendment to the states, and, when Roosevelt took office, it was a foregone conclusion that before long the Prohibition era would be over. But the new administration, reflecting the public mood, urged upon Congress in the meantime the passage of a law legalizing the sale of light wines and beer, and the Congress responded—in the House without even a roll call. The passage of this law marks the end of an attempted reform, and should be listed among those measures of the administration well received by a large part of the business class.

The measures just cited, taken altogether, gave a considerable lift to American morale. But the truly ambitious project of the "Hundred Days" was the National Industrial Recovery Act. This, like the legislation just mentioned, is not to be regarded as in any way an evidence of a swing toward radicalism. On the contrary, it owed its origin, at least in part, to the activities of the United States Chamber of Commerce and was, indeed, the major contribution of the business classes to the problem of the Depression. The period of the twenties had seen the rapid growth of trade associations, that is, combinations of businessmen for the exchange of information, for the improvement of marketing methods, for the establishment of standards and grades, for the fixing of fair trade practices, and in some instances for the actual fixing of prices. But the agreements made in a period of prosperity hardly survived adversity. Under severe pressure the effort at co-operation broke down, ruthless competition ensued, and a dog-eat-dog fight on the part of many firms to get what they considered their fair share of sales demoralized the market. Essentially, what the advocates of the N.I.R.A. proposed was a restoration of orderly methods and agreements to restrict competition and to fix the conditions of labor and of sales prices in industry. The project was a very far-reaching one; it was a wide departure from the notion of a free economy; it suggested what the Europeans described as cartelization. However, it had the support, let us say again, of important members of the business class who were at a later time to become more and more hostile to the New Deal.

But the National Recovery program was viewed by the President from a somewhat different point of view. He indorsed the idea because it commanded widespread support not only among the friends of capital but on a broader basis. In his mind it envisaged the friendly co-operation of industry and labor and staved off legislation of a much more radical character.

The Depression had naturally produced great distress among workers, and the year 1933 saw a powerful agitation for the shortening of the workweek. As early as December, 1932, Senator Black of Alabama had introduced a bill that would limit the hours of work in factories to thirty hours a week. Early in January President Green of the American Federation of Labor, hardly a flaming radical by temperament, had threatened a general strike if legislation of this type were not adopted. In early April of 1933 the Senate suddenly passed the Black Bill, and there were signs that similar action might take place in the House. Obviously, if it went to the White House, a most embarrassing situation would be created. A veto would alienate labor; approval would rouse the businessmen, from whom howls of rage were already resounding at the mere thought of such a measure.

The administration was equal to the situation. The President had astonished Raymond Moley in the campaign of 1932 by asking him to "weave together" a speech with a strong protectionist bias and yet slanted toward reduction of the tariff. Roosevelt now proposed "to weave together" the views of labor and capital. By meeting the demands of the businessmen for codes of fair competition and by combining this with protection for the worker in the form of minimum wages and reasonable restrictions on the hours of labor, it might be possible to produce a statute that would satisfy both sides and lay a broad foundation for business recovery. Early in May, 1933, he appeared before the United States Chamber of Commerce. His speech suggested the legislation that was to come, and it was received with considerable enthusiasm. The Chamber indorsed the general principles of the N.I.R.A. By May 15 a bill had been drafted and sent to Congress. This far-reaching measure exempted from the operation of antitrust laws those business groups to be formed under the new law. It permitted these groups to draw up codes for their own industries subject to governmental approval. It provided punishment for violators of these codes. At the same time, it stipulated for the establishment of minimum wages and maximum hours under the new agreements. Most important of all from the point of view of labor, it guaranteed the right of collective bargaining with employers through representatives freely chosen by the employees.

This last provision was a masterpiece of equivocation. It by no means signified full recognition of the organized trade union. It was drafted in such terms as to leave the way open for the company, or industry-controlled, union as well. It was to cause much trouble in the future, but it is a fair sample of the process of compromise that lay behind much of the legislation of the New Deal.

The President was, for the time, highly content with this solution of his problem. The Blue Eagle, the signal of obedience to and observance of the codes, was put on display throughout the land. In many of the cities, workers and industrialists, even college professor and ministers, marched to the tune of martial music in celebration of the Recovery Act. General Hugh Johnson, ebullient and profane friend of Bernard Baruch, was put in charge of the administration of the measure, and soon the atmosphere was filled with his adjurations and warnings. Codes were rapidly drawn up and put into force. In the view of the administration, we repeat, a great national effort was under way, an effort far transcending partisanship or any rightist or leftist creed.

But with the N.I.R.A., the description of the last of the measures acceptable to a substantial proportion of the business interests must be brought to an end. In the contrary category, generally speaking, must be put the Agricultural Adjustment Act, the handling of the monetary problem, the establishment of the Tennessee Valley Authority, and the administration of relief. Let us look at each of these in turn.

There had been a difficult situation for many farmers even in the golden days of the twenties. Agricultural prices had collapsed after the end of World War I and had never fully recovered. The problem of a farm surplus existed during the Coolidge administration, and there were various proposals for dealing with it. But the strong laissez faire bent of the President prevented action. The problem became worse during the Hoover administration. In one of the least intelligent moves of that harassed regime an attempt was made to raise farm prices by buying large quantities of the staple crops off the market, particularly wheat, corn, and cotton. Since no control of production was incorporated in this plan, it had no positive effect whatsoever. By the end of Hoover's term it had cost the government about $360,000,000 and was abandoned.

The Roosevelt administration was committed to deal with the farm problem. As we have already seen, it performed an important public service along sound lines in creating various lending agencies and in helping the farmer liquidate his debts. But such action, in the distressful conditions of 1933, was by no means enough. Accordingly, in the Agricultural Adjustment Act the government went further. In return for a restriction of output by the individual farmers (the heart of the scheme), benefit payments were offered to growers on a variety of staple commodities, cotton, wheat, corn, hogs, tobacco, and rice. To meet the expense of such a program, a processing tax was levied on the staples affected. But it was necessary to do more. The crops for 1933 were already in the ground. As a purely emergency measure the government ordered the plowing under of a fourth of the cotton crop and the slaughter of more than 6,000,000 pigs. A third feature of the law deserves mention. The scale of payments to farmers was based on a complicated formula known as "parity." The principle of this formula was that the farmer would receive for his product a price that "would give agricultural commodities a purchasing power equivalent to the purchasing power of agricultural commodities in the base period, August, 1909–July, 1914."

The act of 1933 was a profound attempt to alter the free system of agriculture that had historically prevailed in the United States. Once the goal of a controlled farm output had been set, Congress, though not encouraged by the administration, went further. In the legislation of 1934 it abandoned in part the voluntary system of allotments and curtailed all production for cotton growers and imposed taxes on all farmers who exceeded their quotas. The Kerr-Smith Act of the same year similarly taxed the sale of tobacco by farmers who did not sign A.A.A. contracts. Such "regimentation" was new to the farm community, and it marks the end of an era. The limitation of output was not unknown in the business world, but limitation of output brought about by a system of governmental rewards and punishments was something else again. Subsidies for *not* producing marked the beginning of a new era in an important part of the economic sector.

The administration's handling of the money problem also marked a distinct breach with the past, and one that was distasteful to many conservatives. The President had begun with an orthodox financial program, imposing economies on a reluctant Congress and appearing to move toward that balanced budget which he had at times advocated in the course of his campaign. But he had never pledged himself explicitly to a dollar containing a fixed quantity of gold, and before long he began to move away from orthodoxy. In so doing, he responded to what was undoubtedly the powerful drift of opinion and sought rather to control than to resist the tide of sentiment rising in Congress.

There was certainly nothing novel about the clamor for rising prices in the spring of 1933. The history of the United States is filled with demands of this kind, of which perhaps the silver campaign of 1896 is the most remarkable expression. The decline of values in the Depression had been catastrophic. An immense demand was certain to arise for currency manipulation of one kind or another. In the middle of April a proposal by Senator Wheeler of Montana for the free coinage of silver at the ratio of 16 units to 1 of gold was defeated by only 43 to 33, and word came to the administration that many senators had cast their votes against the measure reluctantly. With these warning signs before him, the President signified his willingness to approve a substitute measure which gave him much freedom of action in dealing with the monetary question. The Thomas amendment to the A.A.A. authorized the Chief Executive to take any or all of three measures: to coin silver at 16 to 1, to issue paper money, or to change the gold content of the dollar. The last of these expedients was soon put into practice.

The Two Phases of the Early New Deal

Of the three choices offered him, the President undoubtedly chose the most desirable. The coinage of silver, in the judgment of most economists, made little sense. The issuance of paper money would be regarded by many people with hostility. The manipulation of the gold value of the dollar could be, at least in some measure, justified. Great Britain had gone off gold in 1931. The experiment with managed money had produced no catastrophe in that country; indeed, it had resulted in some positive gain. In the United States it was hoped that revaluation would lead to a rise in prices and that it would stimulate foreign trade. Once the expedient of monetary management had been invoked elsewhere, a case could be made for adopting a similar policy here.

The action of the administration in abandoning the old gold standard, however, could bring nothing but gloom to tradition-minded conservatives. Lewis Douglas, the President's Director of the Budget, found in this measure "the end of Western Civilization." Other friends of the President were almost as much shocked. The definite decision of the government to embargo gold exports, taken on April 19, undoubtedly did something to undermine the orthodox businessman's confidence in the administration. What followed was still less reassuring to the conventional. For some time the President allowed the dollar to float in the exchange markets to find its own level. But when this technique failed to bring about a satisfactory and sustained recovery, Roosevelt went further. He was attracted to a theory brought forward by two Cornell professors which maintained that a further improvement could be brought about by bidding up the price of gold. Secretary of the Treasury Henry Morgenthau was devoted to the President, was a neighbor of his at Hyde Park, and was quite willing to follow where Roosevelt led. For some time, therefore, the two men carried on their experiment while the critics writhed at their method and predicted failure. Failure, indeed, there was. In one of those about-faces that provided excitement for the observer, the administration changed its course again in 1934 and recommended the stabilization of the dollar at a new value in terms of gold. The act of 1934 exists to this day.

As one looks back at the monetary measures as a whole, it is not easy to isolate them from other aspects of the New Deal program and accurately to measure their influence. They may have had some effect in improving our international trade, but they were often met with retaliatory measures that diminished their effect. In the broadest sense, the judgment must be that they were neither so disastrous as their critics suggested nor so efficacious as their sponsors hoped. The notion that tinkering with the price of the precious metals is a sure cure for economic ills finds very inadequate substantiation in this, as in other periods of our economic history.

The financial whimsies of the Roosevelt administration—as they seemed to large elements of the business class—were by no means the only disturbing factors in the administration's policy in 1933. Businessmen often have been reluctant to recognize the necessity for the regulation of their affairs by government. This reluctance proceeds, understandably enough, from their conviction of their own rectitude or from the necessities and pressures of a competitive system. But the history of American economic life suggests clearly that the need for control *does* arise and that the public interest cannot invariably be left to the "natural" operation of economic law.

There had been a flagrant example of this in the speculative orgy preceding 1929, which opened the way for fraud as well as reckless borrowing. It was not strange that among the legislative measures of 1933 was the so-called "truth-in-securities" bill which required that new issues be registered with the Federal Trade Commission and that the most pertinent data with regard to the financial position of the companies be furnished to prospective buyers. But the act was regarded by its enemies as cumbrous and unworkable, and it was revised in 1934, with a Securities Exchange Commission set up to supervise the market. It certainly made few friends for the President in Wall Street.

And there was TVA. To the increasing number of Roosevelt's critics, socialism was inaugurated when the Tennessee Valley Authority Act was passed on May 18. It represented the climax of a campaign that had been waged for years by Senator George Norris of Nebraska. During World War I the government had constructed a dam and two nitrate plants on the Tennessee River at Muscle Shoals, Alabama. After the war an attempt was made to sell these facilities, but no buyers appeared willing to pay more than a tittle of the initial costs. Here were valuable installations capable of producing electric power and fertilizer on a large scale. They were not being utilized. Why should they not be? In particular, in view of the scandals that had been revealed in the field of private-utility administration, why should the government not try its hand? Such was the attitude of the sponsors of the bill. The act passed the Senate by a three-to-one vote early in May and the House by more than two to one. It undoubtedly gave a great impetus to the development of the Tennessee Valley and was hailed by its sponsors as a remarkable piece of regional planning. But here again applause from the masters of capital was muted.

Perhaps the most objectionable measures of the administration, however, lay in the field of relief. This was not true at the beginning. There was little opposition to the idea of a Civilian Conservation Corps, an organization intended to put unemployed youngsters to healthful and fruitful outdoor work at very little more than a minimum wage. Few persons objected very strenuously to the administration's initial policy of grants to the states in place of the loans vouchsafed by the Hoover regime. And there was no widespread hostility to the large public works program, amounting to more than $3 billion, which was one of the features of the N.I.R.A. But no one of these measures went far enough to solve the relief problem. The public works program was in the hands of Secretary of the Interior Harold S. Ickes, one of the most competent administrators of the Roosevelt team. Atrabilious, suspicious, and vain as he undoubtedly was, a "curmudgeon" by his own account, Ickes was unswervingly honest and determined that the program he directed should be administered without fear or favor. In the long run, a great deal was accomplished. But the projects approved by the Public Works Administration did not move fast enough to relieve the widespread unemployment. As 1933 progressed, it was clear that more drastic measures were needed, and the President, as usual, responded to the pressure of the time and the genuine needs of the unfortunate. The public official to whom he turned was Harry Hopkins, soon to become one of his closest and most trusted advisers.

There are few more picturesque figures in the Roosevelt administration than Hopkins. A social worker who enjoyed good living and the company of the well-to-do, a fiercely energetic administrator, though most of the time in precarious health and wracked by pain, idealist and practical politician at the same time— Hopkins brought a very definite point of view to the problem of relief and one that was destined to be accepted by public opinion. He fervently opposed a mere dole; he believed that the unemployed should be given useful work to do. At the outset of the Roosevelt regime he was placed in charge of the Federal Emergency Relief Administration. But this organization worked through local agencies, and from the funds provided by the N.I.R.A. Roosevelt set aside $400,000,000 for a new mechanism, the Civil Works Administration. This program was never intended to be permanent, but in the winter of 1934 the CWA initiated all sorts of projects— road repairs, school improvements, parks and playgrounds, and erosion control. More than 180,000 of these activities were set in motion and more than 4,000,000 people were given employment. Here was a dramatic illustration at first hand of solicitude for the unfortunate through the operation of the federal government itself.

On the whole, as a result of the various policies we have just analyzed—control of agricultural production, the devaluation of the dollar, regulation of the exchanges, TVA, and relief policy— the Roosevelt administration was losing the support of business as the year 1934 advanced. It could not claim, either, that its measures had produced a genuine recovery. Unemployment had declined substantially in the earlier part of 1933 but rose again to 12,000,000 in January, 1934, and was over 11,000,000 in the fall. Industrial production, which had taken a spurt with the N.I.R.A., had slumped and by the end of 1934 had advanced only a third of the way toward the figures of 1929. Agricultural prices, too, though rising, were far below the pre-Depression figures.

Yet in the elections of 1934 the administration scored a sensational victory. Rarely in American history does the party in power increase its congressional representation in a non-presidential election year. But in 1934 the Democrats won 332 seats in the House, as against 313 in 1932, and in the Senate increased their numbers from 50 to 69. How does one explain this fact? The answer to such a question is inevitably complex, but at least some observations can be made. However grim the picture still was in 1934 (and we have just seen that there was no reason for exuberance), the administration by its various measures had convinced a great many groups of its good will. It had intervened actively to deal with the farm problem. It had rescued homeowners and farm owners from bankruptcy. It had won much labor support. And it had made a dramatic and successful appeal to the unemployed. The sympathy and interest of this last-mentioned group was one of its great assets. In particular, the unemployed Negroes of the North, traditionally Republican, were drawn toward the administration. The underprivileged, in general, became the supporters of the Roosevelt regime.

The victory of 1934 was only the beginning of a political process that lasted for more than a decade. The ascendancy of the Democratic party in Congress was to be maintained until 1946, in the Presidency until 1952. And this ascendancy was to rest more and more upon the forces of labor, reinforced by the still solid South and by considerable strength among the western agrarians. On the other hand, the leaders of American capital responded with increasing hostility to the trends in Washington. The period of greatest tension between the President and the American conservatives came in the years 1935–37.

THE "SECOND" NEW DEAL

The objective judgment on the first two years of the New Deal must be a mixed one. The President had met the banking crisis with vigor and with courage; the distress of indebted landowners and homeowners had been in large part alleviated; the administration had shown more solicitude for the hard lot of the unemployed than had its predecessor; something had been done to raise agricultural prices; and a great effort had been launched in the N.I.R.A. Some legislation undoubtedly shocked the orthodox, but the President had made a genuine effort to place his program on a truly national basis and to enlist all economic groups in his

The Two Phases of the Early New Deal

support. But there was another side to the account. There were still millions unemployed at the end of 1934; there had been no restoration of business morale; and the social discontent brought about by the Depression had by no means come to an end.

The dream of a unified nation grappling with the problem of recovery without regard to special interests was to be dissipated in the years 1935 and 1936. The course of events and the circumstances of the time intensified political bitterness, and a swing to the left manifested itself in many ways.

A number of conspicuous individuals personified this drift. There was, for example, such a successful demagogue as bulbous-nosed, vulgar but able Huey Long, who had risen to power in Louisiana as early as 1928, routed the Louisiana Old Guard, and carried through with utter ruthlessness a program of political reform. There were overtones of fascism in Long: his authority, exercised without scruple, far exceeded the bounds of political decency; and from the governor's mansion in Baton Rouge he soon went to the Senate of the United States. By 1934 he had proclaimed a share-the-wealth movement, the principal demand of which was that the government should guarantee an income of $5,000 a year to every family and "make every man a king." There was also Father Coughlin, the priest of the "Little Flower," who had, since early in the Depression, attracted hundreds and thousands of listeners over the radio and who was calling for more inflation and for nationalization of banking and of national resources. There was Upton Sinclair, the writer whose exposures of conditions in the meat-packing industry had stirred many Americans thirty years before. He announced a diffuse program for the ending of poverty, and he nearly won the governorship of California in 1934. And perhaps more important than these, there was Dr. Townsend, an aged doctor who had homesteaded in

Kansas, practiced in the Black Hills, and migrated to California. He came forward with a plan for old age pensions that was truly magnificent in scope. This was based on the idea that every person of sixty years of age of "good character" should receive a stipend of $200 a month from the government on condition that he spend it all before the next payday. The payments were to be financed (inadequately) by a 2 per cent sales tax and, it was calculated, would take nearly half the national income, which would then be turned over to about 8 per cent of the population. Notwithstanding the practical impossibility of such a scheme, Dr. Townsend managed to get a hearing for it. If his testimony is to be believed, something like three thousand Townsend clubs were formed with an average membership of 150 each, clubs which operated in all parts of the country.

Above and beyond all this, the unrest in the ranks of labor had grown rather than declined. The door had been opened to collective bargaining by the N.I.R.A., but it was ajar only, not thrown wide. Powerful John L. Lewis of the coal miners, of burly physique and rotund phrase, egotistical beyond almost any other figure in the labor movement, but shrewd and convinced as to its future, was leading a campaign for the reinvigoration and extension of trade unionism. Even the highly conventional and conservative craft-union leaders, who headed the American Federation of Labor, were becoming more aggressive with the spirit of the times.

How did the President respond to the thunder on the left? The answer to this question lies in a review of the next two years, but some general observations should be made at the outset. Roosevelt certainly did not accept the views of the peddlers of economic nostrums. He certainly did not instigate, as he was later to be charged with doing, the deep discontent felt in the ranks of labor. Despite the criticisms of his enemies, he never really forswore the objective of a balanced budget, though he recognized the need for relief appropriations outside it. He clung with tenacity to the NRA, for him the symbol of co-operative national action, but both his tactical sense and his social sympathies led him to propound a new and positive program.

In so doing, he was more and more led to antagonism toward those who wished to stand pat; in so doing, he cut himself off more and more from the fortunate classes; and in so doing, he aroused an intense resentment among those classes, which was to last for a long time. More than once he was to disclaim any hostility to wealth as such; more than once he was to stress his desire to preserve and not to destroy the capitalist system. The measures that he advocated or approved, however, involved heavier taxation on the well-to-do, greater governmental expenditures, restrictions on the freedom of the business class, and further legislation in the interest of agriculture and labor. It is not strange that they provoked a movement on the right, of which the not very effective prototype was the Liberty League, founded in the fall of 1934 with the object of arresting what its members deemed the alarming drift toward governmental extravagance and the extension of governmental power.

Roosevelt sounded the note of the second two years of the New Deal in his annual message of 1935. "We find," he said, "our population suffering from old inequalities, little changed by past sporadic remedies. In spite of our efforts and in spite of our talk, we have not weeded out the overprivileged, and we have not effectively lifted up the underprivileged. . . . We do not destroy ambition, not do we seek to divide our wealth into equal shares on stated occasions. We continue to recognize the greater ability of some to earn more than others. But we do assert that the ambition of the individual to obtain for him and his a proper security, a reasonable

29

leisure, and a decent living throughout life is an ambition to be preferred to the appetite for great wealth and great power."

First on the list of the definite proposals of the message was a reorganization of the relief administration. Two days after its delivery Roosevelt asked for $4,880,000,000 to be used for giving employment to those on relief rolls. He recommended that this money be borrowed, not raised by taxation. He went on to propose that the federal government assume responsibility for relief through a Works Progress Administration that should have general charge of the expenditure of relief funds. This agency was to provide work for "employables." Those who were unemployable were to be cared for by the states under a program covered in other legislation. The President also set up criteria for projects to be undertaken by the new agency. They should be useful in the sense that they afforded "permanent improvement in living conditions or created future new wealth for the nation; they should be such as involved a large percentage of direct labor; they should be planned and selected to compete as little as possible with private enterprise; they should be so located as to serve the greatest unemployment needs; and they should be compensated for on a scale larger than the amount received as a relief dole, but not so large as to encourage the rejection of opportunities for private employment or the leaving of private employment to engage in government work."

In the months that followed, this ambitious program received the overwhelming approval of Congress. The bill putting it into effect was passed in the House by a vote of 317 to 70 and in the Senate by a vote of 67 to 13. If one attaches any importance whatsoever to the ability of politicians to reflect the public mood, one can say that the new program reflected the preponderant opinion of the American people.

The Two Phases of the Early New Deal

There were, however, few of the New Deal measures that came in for more drastic criticism. In the Senate the administration measure had been amended to provide that all appointments to positions paying more than $5,000 a year should be made with the consent of the Senate itself. This provision was designed to provide political patronage for the members of the upper house, and it gave a political flavor to the administration of the act itself and furnished a talking point for the critics of the measure. It was also charged by the opponents of work relief that there was gross inefficiency in its operation. It is probably true that the workers under the new plan were less efficient than those in private industry; in fact, in at least one case where labor efficiency could be measured, that is, on building projects, it was established that WPA labor was less productive than labor privately employed. But, despite this fact, there can be little doubt that WPA accomplished a great deal during the years it operated.

Under the dynamic leadership of Harry Hopkins it embarked upon a program of infinite variety. Some of its projects were in the field of public construction, some in adult education, some in conservation; some in public health. At the height of its operation more than 3,000,000 people were on the rolls; and, although it is impossible to measure the economic value of all these projects, there is no doubt that they represented a substantial gain to the nation.

One of the most striking features of this program was the attention paid to displaced artists, musicians, actors, and writers. The programs organized to help them did, it is true, come under constant criticism, both from the point of view of the results achieved and from the slant of the social philosophy sometimes expressed in the work done. There were, on the other hand, some distinguished products of these programs in the WPA guides to the states.

The New Age of Franklin Roosevelt, 1932–45

The WPA also established a variety of collateral agencies with special objectives: the Resettlement Administration, intended to take indigent farmers off poor land on which they were struggling to make a living and give them a chance for a new start in life; the National Youth Administration, intended to give unemployed young people a chance for an education or for useful employment; and most significant, the Rural Electrification Administration, which provided loans at low interest and WPA labor to extend power lines to farm homes not served by public utilities.

The WPA was never intended to be permanent. It was designed to deal with a practical situation and one which, it was hoped, would be remedied and would not recur. It undoubtedly strengthened the administration politically. When one considers its scope, one finds it remarkable that it was administered with so little objectionable political activity. The cynical remark attributed to Harry Hopkins that the administration proposed to spend and spend and elect and elect by no means conveys the proper impression of the actual operation of WPA. As we have already seen, the Senate amendment to the WPA appropriation opened the door to political patronage at the higher level. But the corroborated cases of actual corruption or of favoritism in the granting of relief or of the manipulation of recipients for political purposes were by no means numerous. And, if one looks at the matter from a broader point of view, one sees that WPA gave heart to many and utilized idle labor at moderate additional cost over a dole. It so far met with the support of majority public opinion that it was continued until the years of World War II, when reviving prosperity made it superfluous.

More fundamental and more far-reaching than the relief program was the Social Security Act. The United States had lagged behind the great industrial nations of Europe in providing protection against unemployment or provision for old age. Both Great Britain and Germany were far ahead of this country. The laissez faire attitude of the twenties in America, reflected fully as much in the indifference of the labor unions as in the opposition of the business classes, operated to retard what would be almost universally regarded today as one of the most far-reaching and acceptable of the reforms of the Roosevelt period. There were, it is true, some beginnings in the Hoover period. But progress was slow until, in 1934, for the first time in its history, the AF of L, hitherto recorded in opposition, came out in favor of positive action. In the meantime, sentiment for legislation on a national scale was gathering in Congress. Acting cautiously, despite his general sympathy with the idea, President Roosevelt appointed a commission to examine the question and report. It was on the basis of this report that the President recommended legislation in his message of January 17, 1935. After long consideration the Congress responded positively in the act of August 14, which passed the House of Representatives by the crashing vote of 372 to 33 and the Senate by 76 to 6. No measure of the New Deal period received more emphatic approval.

Though the Social Security Act had broader purposes than those of political maneuver, it did take the wind out of the sails of the Townsendites. In the same way, the President moved to discomfit the ebullient Senator Long from Louisiana, whose share-the-wealth program we have mentioned. On June 19 he sent to Congress a message on tax revision in which he declared that "wealth in the modern world does not come merely from individual effort" but "from a combination of individual effort and of the manifold uses to which the community puts that effort." And asserting that "the movement toward progressive taxation of wealth and of income has accompanied the growing diversification and interrelation of effort which marks our industrial society," the President called for inheritance and gift taxes "in respect to all very large amounts received by one legatee or beneficiary" on an increased scale and at the same time urged an alteration of the corporation tax with a reduction of the rates on small businesses and a raising of the rates on large ones. The proceeds from this tax revision, he suggested in what looks very much like a political maneuver to gild the pill, "should be specifically segregated and applied, as they accrue, to the reduction of the national debt." Naturally, there were howls from the right, but when actual legislation followed on the administration proposals, the changes were less dramatic than had been forecast. The tax bill of 1934 had already upgraded inheritance taxes and income taxes. The new law went further, but not so much further as had been feared. For persons with an income of $50,000 the rates were raised by about 1 per cent, with an income of $100,000 by about 6 per cent, and with an income of $3,500,000 by about 16 per cent. Inheritance taxes and gift taxes were increased, less drastically, by about 7 per cent on the very largest fortunes. The changes in the corporation tax were by no means great; all that was done was to ease the tax on small business and raise it slightly on large ones. But there can be little doubt that the passage of the law marked a new step in the hostility of the highly fortunate toward the administration.

But one of the most hotly contested fights of the New Deal era took place when the administration pressed for legislation to deal with the powerful economic interest represented by the power companies. Shrewd manipulators had bought the stock of operating companies and then formed a holding company that in many cases drained the original concerns of their assets and diverted their profits. And in some cases, holding companies had themselves been combined in a super-holding company with a reckless pyramiding of assets. The name of Samuel Insull had become notorious in the

34

Depression period for his reckless operations in this field, leading in time to the collapse of his great empire. The case for legislation was a strong one. Accordingly, the President urged Congress to act on the basis of a report that had been prepared by the Federal Trade Commission and the National Power Policy Committee. The principal feature of this report was a demand for the outright abolition of holding companies which, at the end of five years, could not demonstrate that they were performing useful functions in terms of economies and efficiencies of management. The measure, especially the "death sentence clause," as it was called, provoked a storm of protest from the utilities. It was hotly debated in both houses and passed in August, 1935, only after a compromise provision had been inserted, permitting two levels of holding companies above operating companies. Thus the President's victory was limited.

The measures that we have just considered were all of them in essence a part of the administration program. But the most far-reaching legislation of 1935 was one in which Roosevelt played a wholly subordinate part, even a "cagey" part. This was the Wagner Act which went to the President in July, 1935, and which gave to union labor in the United States a wholly new status.

To understand the Wagner Act, we must go back to the early days of the administration. The American labor movement had been one of the weakest in comparison with that of other highly industrialized nations. The prosperity of the twenties had done nothing to aid it, and the Depression at first resulted in something like demoralization. It was only with the advent of the New Deal that the tide began to turn. The first significant step taken by government with regard to the problem came in the N.I.R.A. of 1933. Passed in the first days of the New Deal, this legislation, as we have seen, attempted to unite the interests of capital and labor in bringing about an economic upturn. For this purpose, the recognition of organized labor brought forth the famous section 7a, which declared that the employees under the codes should "have the right to organize and bargain collectively through representatives of their own choosing and should be free from the interference, restraint, or coercion of employers of labor or their agents, in the designation of such representatives or in self-organization or in other concerted activities for the purpose of collective bargaining or other mutual aid or protection; that no employee and no one seeking employment shall be required as a condition of employment to join any company union or to refrain from joining, organizing, or assisting a labor organization of his own choosing."

That such language should be understood by labor as an invitation to extend its activities is certainly not strange. The straitened conditions in which American workers found themselves had produced a higher degree of labor consciousness than ever before; and the latter part of the year 1933 and still more the spring and summer of 1934 were filled with manifestations of labor unrest. The most dramatic manifestation of this unrest came with the walkout of the longshoremen in San Francisco, which developed into a general strike that lasted for four days. Another example of profound labor disturbance was the North Carolina textile strike in the fall of 1934. Faced with a demand for action from their members, the leaders of the AF of L, long inert so far as the encouragement of union growth was concerned, engaged in more vigorous effort than ever before to increase their numbers and to a substantial degree succeeded.

But large elements in the business classes looked askance at these activities. On the other side of the Atlantic the masters of capital had long since adapted themselves to the fact of labor unions, and a Labor party had in England twice been intrusted with the responsibility of office. But in the United States no such evolution had taken place, and section 7a was taken by many employers as an invitation to hasten the formation of company-controlled unions and to attempt in many ways, some of them none too scrupulous, to circumvent the new development. Confronted with this conflict of interests, the administration pursued a somewhat irresolute course. In August, 1933, it constituted a National Labor Board, headed by Senator Wagner and with three industry and three labor members. But this board soon fell under the displeasure of the employers, largely because of the known interest of the Senator in the cause of labor. In October several companies refused to appear before it, and the National Association of Manufacturers denounced the body's policies as tending to "prevent the prompt and peaceful settlement of industrial disputes." The following month Wierton Steel refused to permit an election under board auspices, and the Budd Manufacturing Company refused to accept its decision. In the winter of 1934 a still more serious controversy broke out. The issue was whether in elections for union representation the majority should be regarded as the representatives of the whole body of employees. When the board attempted to enforce this principle, it found itself opposed by General Johnson, the administrator of the NRA, and his general counsel, Donald Richberg. Faced with the difficult problem of enforcement, the administration tended to draw back. In the industrial disputes of 1934 the President resorted to the technique of special boards for individual industries. Thus in March a special Automobile Labor Board was set up to deal with the touchy situation in that industry and succeeded in averting a walkout. Similar action was taken with regard to the steel industry in June. In July a National Longshoremen's Board brought to an end the strike on the West Coast, and a Textile Relations Board ended the dispute in the southern textile industry.

In the first two of these cases the settlement explicitly provided for recognition of company unions. The President stated with regard to the controversy in the automobile industry, "The Government makes it clear that it favors no particular union, or particular form of employee organization or representation." When Senator Wagner introduced the bill that was to bear his name in its final form, the President requested the Democratic leader, Senator Robinson, to see that it was shelved, and instead a resolution was passed which gave statutory authority to the executive orders issued under the authority of the Recovery Act. In August, 1934, in a gesture that was perhaps intended to propitiate the business interests, the NLB was abolished, and a new National Labor Relations Board was established in its stead.

But the movement for legislation continued to make headway. Robert Wagner was certain of the rightness of his cause. His experience as chairman of the NLB had convinced him that only a law with teeth could properly protect the worker's right to bargain collectively. He pointed out that under the N.I.R.A. great advantages had been given to the employers' associations through the codes but that the labor sections of the act had been largely ineffective. He was undoubtedly influenced in some degree by the stiff-necked attitude that some industrialists had shown toward him personally. He continued to press for a labor law that would go far beyond 7a and provide adequate machinery for enforcement. Simultaneously, the great business groups—the United States Chamber of Commerce, the National Association of Manufacturers, the Iron and Steel Institute—all conducted a strenuous campaign against it.

The President, throughout the winter and spring of 1935, continued to maintain a discreetly cautious attitude. Yet, when the Wagner bill came to a final vote in July, 1935, the measure passed by a large majority, by 63 to 12 in the Senate and without a roll call in the House. In May of that year the N.I.R.A. had been declared unconstitutional by the Supreme Court. The case for the President's signing the Wagner Act was immensely strengthened by this action of the Court, for labor unionism would have been left without any protection whatsoever had the bill been rejected. In a statement exceedingly restrained in tone the President signified his approval.

The National Labor Relations Act reaffirmed the right of workers to bargain collectively through representatives of their own choosing. It created a National Labor Relations Board of three members appointed by the President and confirmed by the Senate. This board was empowered to conduct elections under the law to determine in individual cases the proper bargaining agency, and the agency elected by the majority of the employees as appropriate was to be the exclusive representative of all (an important concession to the labor point of view). A list of unfair practices was compiled, and the board was given authority to issue cease-and-desist orders, which would be enforced, in case of resistance, by the circuit courts of the United States. The findings of the board as to the facts, "if supported by evidence," were declared to be final. The board was given the right to issue subpoenas requiring the testimony of witnesses and the submission of evidence. Failure to comply might be treated as contempt.

No legislation of the New Deal period met with more determined opposition than the Wagner Act. In some striking instances, distinguished lawyers counseled resistance to the legislation on the ground of unconstitutionality. It is safe to say that large elements of the business classes, hitherto critical but not violently hostile to the administration, were alienated by the law. The breach of the administration with a large segment of the employers is signalized by the change in the President's attitude toward the United States Chamber of Commerce between 1933 and 1935. In the first of these years he had spoken to the organization and had been received with great applause. In 1934 he had sent a cordial message. In 1935 he ignored the meeting entirely. Contrariwise, in 1933 both the

Chamber of Commerce and the National Association of Manufacturers had begun with praise of the administration. The tone of both, especially the latter, was more critical in 1934, and by the end of the year the NAM was sharply hostile. Both were distinctly in opposition by 1935.

The Congress of 1935 turned out a grist of legislation that compares with, and perhaps exceeds in significance, that of the "Hundred Days." It wrought far-reaching changes in the activities of government. If the President had not in every case taken the lead in this program, he undeniably found it good. Yet from time to time he made a gesture toward the more conservative elements in the American political scene. One of these was his veto of the bonus bill in May. This measure called for the issuance of an unsupported paper currency to pay off the claims of war veterans to adjusted compensation. It was entirely consistent with Roosevelt's philosophy that he should veto such a measure. He had been opposed to the unrestricted issuance of paper money in 1933. Yet a little something more than this emerged from the veto message. Essentially, the President was saying that unbalancing the budget was justifiable to meet the needs of relief but that reckless finance was to be avoided. Those who thought of him as a mere wastrel could have been a bit comforted by his action in this case.

Again reflecting a more conservative mood was the President's famous letter to the newspaper publisher Roy Howard in the fall of 1935. The publisher, amid many criticisms of the administration, had asked for a breathing spell. The President, declaring that the reform program had now been virtually completed, answered, "The breathing spell is here—very decidedly so." And, if one compares the legislative program of 1936 with that of 1935, one will find some justification for the presidential assurance.

The New Deal, the Courts, and the People

The program of the New Deal, as it had been worked out in 1935, was by no means completed. It depended for its efficacy upon the courts which, in the natural course of events, would be called to pass upon its constitutionality, and by the middle of the year it was obvious that serious difficulties might be met with from the Supreme Court itself. Already there were signs of the development of the struggle that was to come to its height in 1937.

The Supreme Court of the United States exercises a portentous power. In validating—or setting aside—the acts of state legislatures and of Congress it builds its decisions on the precedents. But the Constitution, from the very breadth of its language and from the absence of detail, may be interpreted in more than one way. It would not be right to say that this interpretation is a matter of mere judicial caprice. It *is* fair to say that the social orientation of the judges is bound to have some influence on their construction of American fundamental law.

The Supreme Court of the Roosevelt first term was weighted on the side of a narrow construction of governmental power. Four of the judges, Van Devanter, Sutherland, Butler, and McReynolds, in deciding questions connected with the legislation of the New Deal or similar questions having to do with state legislation of a progressive tenor, were disposed to take the restrictive view. Three others, Cardozo, Brandeis, and Stone, usually inclined to the other side. In the center were Justice Roberts and Chief Justice Charles Evans Hughes. With regard to Roberts, it is difficult to trace in his decisions a coherent judicial theory; with regard to the Chief Justice, it would be right to say that his inclinations lay rather toward broad than toward narrow construction but that, as a jurist steeped in the law, he could not always reconcile New Deal legislation with his judicial conscience. Perhaps, too, he wished to avoid a clear-cut division of the Court into two warring factions.

In the first two years of the New Deal no important cases involving the constitutionality of a federal law were up for decision. A New York State law regulating the price of milk and a Minnesota law providing for a moratorium on debts were sustained, though only by a close vote. But in 1935 congressional statutes came up for review. The first measure to come under close scrutiny was that by which the Congress of 1933 had abrogated the Gold Standard Act of 1900, whereby the government was required to redeem its obligations in dollars of a fixed quantity of gold. A similar requirement had sometimes been inserted in private contracts, and the validity of these contracts was also at stake. The Court sustained the action of the government; but it did so by only a 5-to-4 vote, and the language of the decision with regard to *public* contracts suggested a breach of faith on the part of the administration. Critics of the tribunal were quick to point out that indescribable confusion would have occurred with regard to a host of money questions if the judgment had been unfavorable to the government and that a great and fundamental question of public policy hung by a hair.

The New Deal, the Courts, and the People

Following on the Gold Clause cases came a series of still more disturbing decisions. On May 6, by a 5-to-4 vote and with Chief Justice Hughes vigorously dissenting, the Court set aside a railway retirement act, declaring that the institution of a pension system for railway employees was not warranted under the commerce clause. Three weeks later, on what came to be known by the friends of the administration as Black Monday, three decisions were handed down that aroused further resentment at the White House. The invalidation of the Frazier-Lemke Act, aimed at the relief of farm debtors, involved a measure that had not had the direct sponsorship of the President. In a second case, however, the Court directly challenged the use of executive power, deciding that it was outside the bounds of presidential competence to remove on grounds of political incompatibility a member of the Federal Trade Commission. In the third, the most fundamental, the judges struck down the N.I.R.A.

It is to be noted that in all three of these cases the Court was unanimous. It was not alone judges like McReynolds, the bête noire of the reformers, who took the negative view. It was also Stone and Cardozo and Brandeis, the darlings of the "liberals."

None of the decisions appears shocking in retrospect. In invalidating the moratorium law, the Court's decision suggested, not that *any* such law would be invalid, but that the specific legislation was not sufficiently heedful of the interests of creditors. In denying to the President the right to remove a Federal Trade commissioner, the Court was protecting an administrative agency from executive interference. In the case of the N.I.R.A., the decision did not completely exclude the possibility of self-regulation of business through codes but struck particularly at Congress' delegation of power to the executive to make such codes legally binding. In addition, in justification of its action in this case, it seems entirely likely that the Court only hastened the demise of the Recovery Act. The measure was to expire in two years and would soon have had to come up for renewal. It can hardly be described in retrospect as a success. It had been difficult to enforce compliance with the codes; the Recovery administration had interpreted collective bargaining in such a way as to alienate the trade unions; there were more persons unemployed in May, 1935, than in May, 1934; the act had had only a limited success in raising real wages; and it had been anything but popular with small businessmen. Speaking more broadly, one can say that it was opposed to the fundamental streak of individualism in the American character.

But whatever might be said for the Court's decision, it carried little weight with the President. In three successive press conferences he made his resentment clear, declaring that the Court in its construction of the Constitution had brought the country back to the "horse and buggy age."

Worse was to come. In the January session of 1936 the Court laid low the A.A.A. By this act taxes had been levied on the processors of various agricultural products, and benefit payments to growers were to be paid from these taxes. The Court declared these taxes invalid. They were invalid, the majority of the Court reasoned, because the benefit payments were invalid, and the benefit payments were invalid because Congress had no power under the Constitution to make grants to individuals in order to persuade them to a given course of action, that is, in this case, restriction of their acreage. The Court then went on to generalize with regard to the farm problem; in the words of Mr. Justice Roberts, "Congress has *no power* to enforce its commands on the farmer to the ends sought by the Agricultural Adjustment Act. It does not help to declare that ocal conditions throughout the nation have created a situation of national concern; for this is but to say that wherever there is a widespread similarity of local conditions, Congress may ignore constitutional limitations upon its own powers and usurp those reserved to the states." The Court went even further. Asserting a point of view with which few specialists in constitutional law would agree today, it maintained the hoary doctrine that all that the Court did was to lay the statute beside the Constitution and provide a completely objective answer. In other words, in the view of the majority, the decision was inescapable.

Three of the Supreme Court justices did not think so. Few dissents in the history of the Court have been so vigorous or so charged with feeling as that which Justice Stone rendered in the A.A.A. case. "Courts are not the only agency," wrote the Justice, "that must be assumed to have capacity to govern. Congress and the Courts both unhappily may falter or be mistaken in the performance of their constitutional duty. But interpretation of our great charter of government which proceeds on any assumption that the responsibility for the preservation of our institutions is the exclusive concern of any one of the three branches of government, or that it alone can save them from destruction is far more likely in the long run to obliterate the constituent members of an indestructible union of indestructible states than the frank recognition that language, even of a constitution, may mean what it says; that the power to tax and spend includes the power to relieve a nationwide economic maladjustment by conditional gifts of money."

The decision of the Court in the A.A.A. case not only aroused sharp criticism among the dissenting justices, but it created very serious practical difficulties. Its suggestion that agricultural surpluses were no concern of government was one that, if followed to its logical conclusion, would render the government impotent to deal with a pressing problem. The decision also struck a blow at the federal budget. "Nearly a billion dollars," wrote Robert Jackson, then Solicitor-General and later a member of the Court, "had been collected from processors under a law which was now held to be unconstitutional, and the always over-burdened Treasury faced immediate demand for refunds of this amount. Nor was this the worst. Those who technically could claim the refund of these taxes had in many, perhaps in most, instances already collected the tax from the consumer by passing it on in the price of their products. Those who stood to collect a billion in refunds from the United States Treasury were those who had not actually borne the burden of the tax. Processing companies stood to be unjustly enriched to the tune of a billion dollars. Having collected the taxes once out of their customers, to recollect them from the government was a clear windfall. . . . The problem of tax refunds thrown upon the government by the Supreme Court, in the magnitude of the sums involved, and in the number and conflicting equities of the persons affected, was without precedent in any nation."

It is right to say that the problem alluded to by Jackson was satisfactorily solved in part by a congressional act that required processors, in order to claim a refund, to prove that they had themselves borne the tax. But the Court complicated the matter by another decision. A large number of court orders (1,600) against payment of the tax had been granted in the district courts in the interest of the processors. Those who instigated these suits could have added, and often did add, to their sales price the tax itself. If the injunctions stood, they could keep this amount. On the Monday following the A.A.A. decision the Court sustained the injunctions and this in disregard of numerous precedents and of a statute which provided that "no suit for the purpose of restraining the assessment or collection of any tax shall be maintained in any Court." In 1938 one of America's most distinguished authorities in the field of constitutional law, Professor E. W. Corwin of Princeton, wrote: "The gradual strangulation of this provision [i.e., the statute just alluded to] in recent years makes a most extraordinary chapter in the history of judicial power, the latest phase being the award by the Court of some $200,000,000 to people most of whom were probably not entitled to it."

On April 1, 1936, the Court handed down a decision with regard to the activities of the Securities Exchange Commission. One Jones had filed a registration statement with the commission in regard to certain oil royalties. When the truth of his assertions was questioned, he sought to withdraw his statement. The commission attempted to persist in its investigation, and Jones resisted. The question before the Court was whether Jones's withdrawal deprived the regulatory authority of any right to proceed further. There were certainly two possible points of view with regard to this matter; but what was remarkable in the 6-to-3 decision of the Court in favor of Jones was the strong language of the majority. The position of the commission was described as "unreasonable and arbitrary." It was compared with the "intolerable abuses of the Star Chamber." On the other hand, Justice Cardozo, writing for the minority, declared: "The argument lays hold of strange analogies. A Commission which is without coercive powers, which cannot arrest or amerce or even punish for contempt . . . is likened with denunciatory fervor to the Star Chamber of the Stuarts. Historians may find hyperbole in the sanguinary simile." Such divergences of opinion made it clear that within the Court itself sharp divisions of feeling as well as of reason had made themselves felt.

During this same month came another decision which struck down an administration-sponsored statute. After the ending of the N.I.R.A., Congress had attempted to draw up a law on the same general principles for the coal industry alone. From the beginning there must have been grave doubt of its constitutionality and sharp criticism of the enactment, and of the President's sponsorship of it on that ground. But there seemed to the legislators to be a possible difference between codes that regulated wages and codes that regulated prices. The former might be invalid and yet the latter might be sustained under the congressional power to regulate commerce. Accordingly, the Guffey Coal Act was divided into sections, and it expressly stipulated that unfavorable judicial action on one of these sections [i.e., the wage section] should not affect another. Notwithstanding this, when the case came before the Court, five of the judges struck down the whole statute. Chief Justice Hughes led the dissenters in an opinion moderately phrased. But Justice Cardozo, in a separate opinion, wrote, after painting a picture of the chaos in the coal industry: "Congress was not condemned to inaction in the face of price wars and wage wars so pregnant with disaster. Commerce had been choked and burdened; its normal flow had been diverted from one state to another; there had been bankruptcy and waste and ruin alike for capital and for labor. The liberty protected by the Fifth Amendment does not include the right to persist in this anarchic riot."

One more decision of the Court in the year 1936 must be mentioned. Here the legislation of the Roosevelt administration was not directly involved, but the spirit of the New Deal was challenged. The state of New York had passed a law fixing a minimum wage for women employed in certain types of industrial establishments. The operator of a laundry brought suit under the Fourteenth Amendment, claiming that the regulation of wages was a violation of that clause of the amendment which declares that no state shall deprive any person of life, liberty, or property without due process of law. There followed a highly important litigation in which many other states besides New York joined in support of the law and in which employers' associations filed briefs against it. The Court divided 5 to 4. Basing itself upon a decision rendered in 1923 with regard to a minimum wage law in the District of Columbia, the so-called Adkins case, the majority of the judges found the statute unconstitutional. "The state is without power," they declared, "by any form of legislation to prohibit, change, or nullify contracts between employers and women workers as to the amount of wages to be paid." On the other hand, Justice Stone, speaking for the minority, wrote: "There is grim irony in speaking of the freedom of contract protected by the Fourteenth Amendment of those who, by their economic necessities, give their services for less than is needful to keep soul and body together. But if this is freedom of contract, no one has ever denied that it is freedom which may be restrained, notwithstanding the Fourteenth Amendment, by a statute passed in the public interest." He pointed out with some force that twenty-one countries had enacted minimum wage legislation and that seventeen states had done the same. "It is difficult to imagine any grounds," he went on, "other than our own personal economic predilections for saying that the contract of employment is any the less an appropriate subject of legislation than are scores of others, in dealing with which this Court has held that legislatures may curtail individual freedom in the public interest. . . . We have had the opportunity to perceive more clearly (since 1923) that a wage insufficient to support the worker does not visit its consequences upon him alone; that it may affect profoundly the entire economic structure of society, and, in any case, that it casts on every tax-payer and on government itself, the burden of solving the problems of subsistence, health and morals of large numbers of the community. Because of their nature and extent these are public problems. A generation ago they were for the individual to solve; today they are the burden of the nation."

The minimum wage decision aroused much public criticism. In

conjunction with the Adkins case (which involved a federal statute), it seemed to bar the door to state and congressional legislation alike. It seemed to place a permanent barrier in the way of any attempt to deal with an important problem by legislative means. That the President should have pointed this out in one of his press conferences was to be expected.

The Supreme Court decisions of 1935 and 1936 seemed to both conservatives and liberals alike to threaten the foundations of the "Second New Deal." But the President, despite his expressed discontent and the discontent of many of his close advisers, such, for example, as Harold Ickes, was too cautious to propose any action at this time. On the contrary, he proposed to build up his fences for the presidential campaign that was just ahead. The session of 1936, though by no means distinguished by such a spate of legislation as that of 1935, was such as to strengthen the administration for the forthcoming election.

By far the most important measure of this session was the so-called Soil Conservation and Adjustment Act for the benefit of agriculture, passed within two months of the Supreme Court decision in the A.A.A. case. This bill was in form no more than an amendment to a soil conservation act passed in the preceding year. However, it provided for benefit payments to farmers who took part of their land out of the cultivation of soil-depleting crops and grew instead crops which would restore the soil. This was, of course, another way of accomplishing the ends proposed by earlier legislation, since the list of crops to be restricted was very much the same as that for which subsidies were granted in the legislation of 1933. But there was, perhaps, a sounder idea behind this later statute, and whether there was or not, it produced much satisfaction in the farm belt and was followed by rising prices.

Other legislative measures of the session of 1936 did something to win the voters. The N.I.R.A., though the product of business thinking, had always been more popular with the large than with the small entrepreneurs. It had probably been of more advantage to the former, also, in practice. The proper answer to the Supreme Court decision, therefore, from the political point of view, was to do something for the small businessman. The Wealth Tax Act of 1935, already mentioned, was a gesture in this direction. Two more measures passed in 1936 were similar in purpose. One, directed against the chain stores, forbade business concerns to charge different prices to different customers unless the costs were different. Another, the Miller-Tydings Act, was directed against cutthroat competition by permitting manufacturers to fix minimum retail prices for their products.

None of the measures would have availed, it may be presumed, if the campaign year of 1936 had not been a year of very substantial economic recovery. By June, industrial production had recovered nearly to the level of 1923–25. Factory employment had gone from 64 to 85, factory payrolls from 46 to 76. Farm prices, with an index of 100 for 1926, had risen from 58 in June, 1932, to 78; unemployment, still more than 10,000,000 in the winter of 1936, had, according to the National Conference Board figures, shrunk to about 6,000,000 in June; the national income, which had fallen to $44 billion in 1932, was rising and was to reach $65 billion for the year as a whole. With such an agreeable turn of the tide, it was not unnatural that the administration should abstain from advocacy of sweeping change. Only an undistributed profits tax on corporate revenues awakened the criticism of the business interests and expressed the New Deal theory of forcing more and more money into the economic blood stream.

When it came to the campaign of 1936, in so far as the Democratic party was concerned, there could be only one course of action, the renomination of the President. When the nominating convention met, an appeal was made to the delegates by former New York Governor Alfred E. Smith, the candidate of 1928, and by some other dissentients to substitute for Roosevelt "some genuine Democrat, if you are to show yourselves fit to follow in the footsteps of Jefferson, Jackson and Cleveland." But this appeal to the past was without effect. The President was nominated by acclamation, and when he came from Washington to accept the nomination, he was received with the wildest enthusiasm.

The Democratic platform was more notable for its claims than for its promises. It contained remarkably few commitments for the future. Significantly, it promised a balanced budget "at the earliest possible moment." It hinted at the idea of a housing program; it pledged vigorous enforcement of the laws against monopoly (a marked change from the spirit of 1933 and a gesture to small business) it approved (as who would not?) "the objective of a sound currency." It laid stress on the important role of the national government in dealing with the problems of wages, maximum hours, child labor, and working conditions in industry. On the touchy question of the Court it was cautious. "If these problems cannot be effectively solved by legislation within the Constitution, we shall seek such clarifying amendments as will assure to the legislatures of the separate states and the Congress of the United States, each within its proper jurisdiction, the power to enact those laws which the state and Federal legislatures, within their respective spheres, shall find necessary, in order adequately to regulate commerce, protect public health and safety and safeguard economic security." It also contained the almost traditional denunciation of the Republican party as the party of special privilege.

The Republicans had held their convention in advance of the Democrats. There was no conspicuous personality who could be

The New Deal, the Courts, and the People

put at the head of the ticket against the President. There could be no question of the renomination of Herbert Hoover, so crushingly defeated in 1932. What was done, in accordance with the exigencies of the occasion, was to nominate a fairly colorless candidate, Alf Landon, who had not expressed himself very vigorously in opposition to the New Deal, who came from the Middle West where the Republican farm vote had been traditionally strong, and who had a creditable record as the governor of his own state of Kansas. His mildly progressive background included support of Theodore Roosevelt in 1912. Landon made a vigorous campaign, but he was not widely known, and, as the event was to prove, he was quite incapable of firing the imagination of the voters or of sharpening the issues.

That the Republican platform should denounce the Democrats was to be expected. This is standard party practice. But the thing to look for in the party declarations of the opposition is not what they condemn but what they concede. For, by observing these concessions, one can trace the movement of public opinion and measure the degree to which the reforms of the preceding four years have been generally or in large degree assimilated. From this point of view, it is worth noting that the Republicans indorsed the principle of old age and unemployment payments, though proposing a general direct tax rather than the method of the law of 1936. They pledged themselves (and it is striking that they did so) to "protect the rights of labor to organize and to bargain collectively through representatives of its own choosing without interference from any source." They indorsed minimum wage laws and minimum hours laws for women and children (this despite the attitude of the Supreme Court). "We believe," the platform stated hopefully, "this can be done within the Constitution as it now stands." The plank dealing with agriculture indorsed the soil conservation program laid down in congressional legislation, suggesting that that program might be better administered. There was a strong declaration against monopoly. All in all, there were clear signs that something of the New Deal had been accepted even by its opponents.

At the same time, the temper of the platform differed from that of the party in power. There was in it a distrust of federal power and there was strongly implied criticism of the pump-priming process which lay behind the large expenditures on relief and which, so the Democrats would claim, was largely responsible for recovery. The conservative instincts of the business classes find their reflection in its language.

At the very opening of the campaign and again at its close President Roosevelt launched a vigorous attack on those whom he chose to describe as "economic royalists." In his own view his administration had built on a broader basis than its predecessor. It had sought to reflect the interest of the farmer and the worker, and it had at the same time brought about a substantial measure of recovery in the field of business as well. The administration had been fought, the President declared, by special interests anxious to maintain their privileged position and determined to resist the institution of necessary controls. To his opponents, Roosevelt's language seemed like an incitement against the business class as a whole, an unnecessary stressing of the theme of class conflict, a discreditable political maneuver. Whether this second view had any validity or not, it seems likely that however the President had carried himself, he would have been elected. He scored one of the most crashing victories in the history of American politics. He received the greatest number of votes any presidential candidate had ever received and the greatest percentage of the popular vote scored by any candidate. He carried every state except Vermont and Maine. He gained more than two-thirds of the total vote, not only in the South

The New Deal, the Courts, and the People

but in the border states, the Rocky Mountain states, and on the Pacific slope. The scope of his victory was the more astounding since it was, by many people, unexpected. The *Literary Digest* poll, for example, hitherto a fairly reliable prophet of election trends, had forecast Landon's election.

In the face of figures so astounding, it is impossible to trace the President's victory to any single force. A part of the answer lies in the efficiency of the party organization. James A. Farley, Postmaster-General and chairman of the Democratic National Committee, was undeniably one of the great political organizers of modern times. He had been discovered by Roosevelt at the outset of his first term as governor, had become chairman of the New York State Committee in 1930, and had moved to the national chairmanship in 1932. Gum-chewing, affable to a degree, an inveterate correspondent on a scale almost unprecedented (his green-ink letters became famous), he was ideally equipped for his post. He kept his finger on the pulse of the Democratic organization in every state in the Union and contributed to the Roosevelt victory by his emollient personality and by the shrewd distribution of patronage.

But much as every candidate needs an experienced political mechanician, it is never wise to attribute a great party victory to mere manipulation. Roosevelt won because he appealed to numerous important segments of the population. In particular, he owed much to the industrial workers and to the powerful body, founded in the fall of 1935 by secession from the American Federation of Labor, which called itself the Committee for Industrial Organizations and which, under the leadership of John L. Lewis, vigorously contended for the Democrats. Along with this support he had a powerful following among the farmers, among those on relief, and in some degree among the small businessmen. Finally, he was assisted—vitally assisted—by the fact that 1936 was the high point of the recovery under the New Deal. It is difficult to argue with the voters as to the necessity of a change when things are going right economically (though the rule has exceptions, as was to be proved in 1952).

One of the interesting features of the campaign of 1936 is the manner in which it reflects the limited character of political discontent on the left. The Communist party vote dropped to a paltry 80,000 in a vote of more than 44,000,000. The Socialists plummeted from nearly 900,000 to less than 200,000. An ephemeral party of protest in which Gerald L. K. Smith, the heir of Huey Long, and Father Coughlin had had a leading part and which was headed by Congressman Lemke of North Dakota accumulated less than a million votes, of which more than a third were concentrated in three states. Once again the American people had shown their traditional loyalty to the two-party system and their preference for experimentation and reform over doctrine.

In one sense, however, the figures just given may be misleading, especially with regard to communism. Though the Communist vote was small, the Communist influence among intellectuals and in the trade unions was not insignificant at this time. The temper of the period was reformist, and naïve and inexperienced members of the intelligentsia no doubt fell for the Communist argument in larger numbers than appears on the surface. The New Deal to them seemed to have no coherent program; the alleged immunity of the Soviet Union from depression attracted them to the regime in Moscow. The labor movement, too, looking for assistance in its struggle for power, found the Communists useful allies. Add to this the fact that the Soviet Union in 1936 was minding its manners, acting with caution in international affairs, and adopting a fake democratic constitution at home, and one gets a still fuller explanation of a subterranean sympathy with Moscow. That sympathy was, of course, wholly misguided; in many cases disillusionment came before the end of the decade; but its existence is a fact that cannot be denied. On the other hand, it is clear that the mass of the people in 1936 repudiated, as they have always repudiated, extreme courses and found satisfaction in voting for a candidate of one of the traditional parties.

III

The New Deal Weakens

The electoral victory of 1936 represents in one sense the height of the New Deal. The next two years were to see no such spate of new legislation as had characterized Roosevelt's first term. They were to see, also, a defeat for the President on one of his most important proposals, his failure to refashion the Democratic party along the lines of his own preferences, and a receding of the Democratic political tide. Although the reforming instinct was not exhausted, it was obviously losing a part of its force.

It was the President himself who introduced division into the Democratic ranks almost immediately after the election. He did so by putting forward proposals for the reform of the Supreme Court.

That the decisions of the Court in 1935 and 1936 should have awakened resentment in the White House was natural enough. That the question of "dealing with" the Court should have been discussed in the inner circles of the administration was equally natural. But no hint of what was to come was given in the presidential campaign, for the president kept his own counsel. Only when the struggle was over, and after preparation so secret that the congres-

The New Deal Weakens

sional leaders themselves were in ignorance of what was to come, did he present the court-packing plan to the Congress. To the general public it was a complete surprise.

The President's message of February 5, 1937, was based upon the theory that the courts were behind in their work, and the assault upon the Supreme Court was masked in more general suggestions for the reform of the judiciary. The President proposed that, when any judge of any federal court who had been on the bench more than ten years failed to resign six months after his seventieth birthday, the President might appoint a sort of co-adjutor for him in the same court. Second, he proposed that additional judges might be appointed but that the number of the judges of the Supreme Court might not be increased by more than six. Third, he proposed that the Chief Justice might assign extra circuit judges to any circuit court of appeals that was behind in its work. Fourth, he proposed that the Supreme Court might appoint a proctor to watch over the process of litigation and investigate the need for assigning additional justices as required.

The issue involved in this plan was a far-reaching one. Assuming (what was true) that the Court had stood in the way of many of the New Deal laws (and this by a narrow majority) and that it had sustained others only by a narrow margin, was it desirable by a new act of legislation to swamp the so-called "reactionary" judges and, by the addition of new members to the Court, insure a more hospitable reception to the New Deal legislation of the future? That such a project was constitutional in the narrow sense of the term few could question, for the right of Congress to fix the size of the Court had long been recognized. But were there deeper considerations involved? Was it fundamentally desirable to reshape the Court and to undermine its independence as a result of a political victory? Or, in the longer view, did such action create more problems than it solved? These issues were heatedly discussed in the course of the year 1937. Opposition began to gather from the day the message was read, and this opposition came not only from the die-hard conservatives but from many liberals who recognized the difficult situation created by the previous decisions of the Court and who, in some instances, were pondering upon some way to meet the problem. The leader of the Senate group in taking up the cudgels against Roosevelt was Burton K. Wheeler of Montana, who had helped carry the holding companies bill through Congress and who had voted for a great deal of the New Deal program. A great legislative struggle seemed to impend. The indirection with which Roosevelt approached the Court issue was quickly capitalized by Chief Justice Charles Evans Hughes. In Hughes the President met a foeman worthy of his steel. Intellectually of the first order, learned in the law, with a shrewd tactical sense, profoundly shocked by the court-packing plan, Hughes quickly seized the advantage and in a famous letter tore to shreds the sophistical argument that the Supreme Court was behind in its work. But this in itself would not have been enough to defeat the proposal. The crucial matter was that, shortly after the Senate committee began its hearings on the President's bill, the Court handed down two fateful decisions which demonstrated that the constitutional law of the United States was keeping pace with the times.

The first, the case of *West Coast Hotel* v. *Parrish*, found constitutional a minimum wage law enacted by the state of Washington. The vote was 5 to 4. Justice Roberts, who had voted against sustaining the New York law the year before on the ground that the state had failed to distinguish the statute from the minimum wage law invalidated in the Adkins case in 1923, now was ready frankly to overrule the previous decision. More important, a week later, the Court upheld the Wagner Act, again by a 5-to-4 vote, in the

The New Deal Weakens

famous case of *Jones and Laughlin Steel Companies* v. *National Labor Board*. The decision in this case was phrased in very broad terms. It not only sustained the most controversial of all pieces of New Deal legislation, but it also foreshadowed the acceptance by the Court of such important statutes as the Social Security Act of the same year.

The decision of the Court in these two cases eviscerated the President's supporters. But more was to come. In June one of the four conservative judges, Justice Van Devanter, resigned. The opponents of the court-packing plan had pushed through Congress a law which assured retiring justices full pay after retirement. Van Devanter took advantage of this provision. The President was thus in a position to appoint a justice, the first since he had entered office. Thus the argument for the bill was weaker than ever. Though the presidential pressure continued, in July the whole project was abandoned.

The thick-and-thin supporters of Franklin Roosevelt have been accustomed to assert that if the President lost the battle, he won the war, that if his legislation failed, he had the satisfaction of seeing the Court bend to the spirit of the times. But apart from the fact that there was a fundamental issue involved in the court-packing plan itself, and one on which the President lost, it is impossible to prove that the plan was actually responsible for the shift in the Court's position. Chief Justice Hughes stoutly denies this in his autobiographical notes and points out that the decision in the minimum wage case preceded the message to Congress. As for Justice Roberts, the swing-man in the whole matter, may he not have been influenced by the election of 1936? Did it need additional pressure to bring him around? And did not the fact that Hughes warmly praised his switch on the minimum wage case, and most assuredly made his associates aware of the magnitude of the issue involved, have something to do with Roberts' concurrence in the later decision on the Wagner Act? Such questions we cannot answer with certitude; but merely to raise them illustrates the danger of dogmatic judgment on the whole problem.

Furthermore, as the late Justice Jackson pointed out, though the Court adjusted itself to the times, in the long run the question raised by the court-packing struggle remains. Judges by their nature and function tend to the conservative point of view. The issues raised in 1937 may easily arise again in the future. The Court may once again, as it has on several occasions in the past, put obstacles in the way of social change. The President had no guaranty from the long point of view.

In still another sense, Roosevelt came out of the Supreme Court struggle as a loser. Public opinion had expressed itself emphatically —and perhaps preponderantly—against him. The strenuous opposition to the court-packing plan suggests—indeed, it may be said to demonstrate—that the majority of the American people accept as desirable the system of constitutional limitations of which the Court is the bulwark. The dropping of the project brought relief in many quarters and to many of the President's usual supporters. In the judgment of a large number of people it was fortunate that the issue was settled in the way it was.

Finally, by the Supreme Court proposal Roosevelt disrupted his own party. The powerful influence that he had exerted over Congress was substantially diminished. He was never again, until America's entry into the war (perhaps not even then) to be as strong at the other end of Pennsylvania Avenue as he had been during his first term.

But to say that the President did not accomplish his purpose, that he was weaker rather than stronger because of the struggle, is not to say that the Court would have been wise had the majority of its judges maintained the attitude which they took in 1935 and 1936. History itself demonstrates that our highest tribunal will suffer grievously in prestige and power if it fails to conform to the spirit of the times. The pro-slavery attitude of the judges in the fifties, and specifically the Dred Scott decision, is witness to this fact. The judicial veto was powerless to stem the tide of opposition to the extension of slavery, and the bloody arbitrament of war reversed the decision handed down from the bench. To the extent that Charles Evans Hughes was responsible for the altered attitude of the Court in 1937, he acted in the highest tradition of judicial statesmanship.

The defeat of the administration on the court-packing plan was by no means its only legislative setback in the session of 1937. Early in the year a few measures reflecting the New Deal spirit were passed. A law intended to deal with the problem of farm tenancy in the South was enacted and received the President's signature. A housing bill, authorizing the loan of federal money for slum clearance, went to the White House. A new coal bill was passed without the hours and wages clauses of the law invalidated by the Supreme Court in 1935. But the far more important measures sponsored by the President failed, failed not only in the regular session but in the special session that he called in November. Congress would have nothing to do with a grandiose plan for the establishment of seven regional authorities to cover the nation with agencies "to conserve and safeguard the prudent use of waters, water power, soils, forests and other resources of the areas entrusted to their charge." It declined to pass agricultural legislation. It failed to carry through on a law fixing maximum hours and minimum wages in industry. And it turned a deaf ear to the President's plea for authority to carry through a great administrative reorganization and clearly showed its reluctance to give to the executive the wide powers he asked in connection with this project.

The New Age of Franklin Roosevelt, 1932–45

There is no doubt that for Franklin Roosevelt the year 1937 was a year of frustration.

There were economic difficulties, too, with which the President had to deal. The year 1937 was one of labor turmoil and one which brought to a head one of the most important social movements in the American economic order. The traditional American labor-union movement had, as we have seen, made very little progress in the twenties and had been shaken by the Depression. It was tied, too, to the system of craft organization in contradistinction with so-called vertical, or industrial, unionism. Even under the N.I.R.A., with its recognition of collective bargaining, the AF of L made relatively little progress. But new forces were operating in the labor movement. John L. Lewis, dominating and domineering, the head of the United Mine Workers for nearly two decades, conducted a successful drive for more complete unionization of the coal industry in 1933. Sidney Hillman and David Dubinsky, leaders in the movement for industrial unionism, pressed forward the organization of the Amalgamated Clothing Workers and the International Ladies Garment Workers. The old guard of the AF of L refused to go ahead, and by 1935 the militant elements in labor unionism had formed a new organization, the Committee for Industrial Organizations. By 1936 the breach between this new group and the Federation became complete, and the CIO began a strenuous effort to organize some of the great industries of the country on the basis of industrial unionism. It was partially successful in the case of steel; in the spring of 1937 United States Steel and a large number of small companies made an agreement with the union without a strike. But the group known as Little Steel—Republic, Bethlehem, Inland, and Youngstown Sheet and Tube—held out, and a bitter ensuing industrial conflict was won (temporarily) by the companies. A more disturbing breach of industrial peace came in the automobile industry. There in January, 1937, sit-down strikes broke out, with the attempt to organize the automobile workers, directed against General Motors. The workers refused either to leave the plants where they were employed or to work. After several weeks of violence the giant automobile company capitulated and recognized the union, and a strike at the Chrysler plants brought the same result. Ford did not come to terms until 1940.

It seems probable that the country had never witnessed such virulent industrial warfare as accompanied these attempts at organization. Both sides resorted to tactics that met with widespread condemnation. The sit-down strikes were declared illegal by the Supreme Court in 1939. On the other hand, a Senate committee under the chairmanship of Senator Robert La Follette of Wisconsin revealed many questionable practices on the part of employers: the use of vigilantes, of labor spies, of threats to workers and their families, and of the use of armed forces to break down labor resistance.

All these events imposed new problems on the administration. In general, its attitude was to try to keep its hands off, and on one occasion Roosevelt expressed what was probably his real attitude with the remark, "A plague on both your houses." But this aloofness seemed, on the whole, to serve the cause of labor, and the government's refusal to use force (particularly in the case of the sit-down strikes) seemed to its critics a shameful abdication of authority. In the Democratic party the more conservative elements became more and more estranged from the White House.

In this most difficult of the Roosevelt years there was trouble of another kind. The year had begun with great prosperity. Since there were inflationary symptoms, the pump-priming policies of 1935 and 1936 were attenuated. The rolls of the WPA were reduced, and the idea of a balanced budget was again put forward. The reserve requirements of the Federal Reserve Banks were increased in an effort to check what appeared to be a full-fledged boom.

But a slump occurred in the summer of 1937. Industrial production fell steeply and farm wholesale prices declined. Unemployment increased from 4,991,000 in August, 1937, to 9,587,000 in May, 1938. The enemies of the administration gleefully pointed to this decline as proof that the Roosevelt policies were a failure. The defenders of the President took the view in many instances that the deflationary measures of 1937 were a mistake and that what had been demonstrated was the necessity for more vigorous pump-priming again.

In the face of these untoward events the President never appeared less resolute than at the opening of 1938. Contrary to what is commonly believed, he had never been an advocate of unlimited expenditure to beat the Depression. He had only insisted that relief for the distressed took a superior place over a balanced budget. He never completely surrendered the hope of arriving at such a budget until the European crisis deepened. In the latter part of 1937 the President clung obstinately to the hope that things would turn out all right and permitted Secretary of the Treasury Henry Morgenthau to make a speech on November 10 pledging an end of governmental deficits. Nor was he apparently at all impressed when John Maynard Keynes, the distinguished British economist, wrote to him in 1938 urging an ambitious program of public works as a way to deal with the deepening crisis. Keynes received only a perfunctory reply prepared for Roosevelt's signature by Morgenthau. Roosevelt was at this time, as always, opportunist rather than wedded to any theory. His mind did not think in abstract terms easily; and it would be quite misleading to picture him as having any coherent financial doctrine during his administration.

The New Deal Weakens

By the spring of 1938 matters had become so much worse that it was necessary to do something. The President recommended new, large-scale appropriations for WPA, and Congress responded. The Depression somewhat strengthened his tactical position, and he was able to secure a part of the legislation (hardly the major part) he had recommended in 1937. After a sharp struggle the congressional leaders secured a minimum wage law. They were also able to do something for the farmer. Indeed, the Agricultural Act of 1938 is an important statute. It replaced the legislation of 1933, declared unconstitutional by the Supreme Court. It was based on the principle of controlled production, as had been the preceding law. A marketing quota could be fixed for the various staple crops and a referendum held for the growers. If two-thirds of them accepted the quota, allotments would be made to each farmer. If the farmer marketed more of the crop than that allotted to him, he was penalized. In addition, loans were to be made to farmers on their produce which could be stored against a possible later shortage. Beyond this, if the price of the regulated commodities fell below a stated percentage of parity, the government would make up all or part of the difference with parity payments to farmers. Judgment of the operation of this statute was soon to be made difficult by the outbreak of the war in Europe and by an increasing and abnormal demand for foodstuffs. But the principle that it embodied was to survive the war itself.

But the passage of the minimum wage law and of the A.A.A. were the only successes which the President enjoyed. Clearly resentful of the diminishing support he was receiving, he embarked upon a course of action which again led to defeat. He determined upon an all-out attack against those conservative Democrats who were blocking his program. If one puts the matter more broadly, one can see that he sought to give to his party a distinctively liberal political flavor and that by abandoning a principle of action which he formerly espoused (abstinence from local contests), he sought to secure the nomination of "liberal" Democrats in the primary campaigns of 1938. He opposed the renomination of such stalwarts as Senator Walter George, one of the most respected members of the Senate, of "Cotton Ed" Smith of South Carolina, another veteran, and of the able Senator Millard Tydings of Maryland. He also sought to displace John O'Connor, a Democratic representative from New York who, as chairman of the powerful Rules Committee of the House, had been able to prevent the passage of the legislation that the President desired. In his efforts to reform his party the President met a resounding defeat. Although O'Connor did not win, the President's other foes did. Moreover, the elections of 1938 brought a substantial diminution of the Democratic membership in the House, for the number shrank from 322 to 262.

The failure of the President to "purge" the Democratic party of its conservatives has a very substantial historical significance. It raises an important question of political philosophy. Would American politics be raised to a higher level if, as is often suggested, the two great political organizations more genuinely represented contrasting points of view, if, to use the conventional terms, one were liberal and the other conservative? There are many who contend so. Such people believe that parties should be organized around principles and that the object of a political debate is to give the electorate a chance to choose between two divergent approaches to the problems of the time. They are repelled by the shufflings and evasions of a political campaign. They believe that it would make for clarity and for sincerity if there were more clear-cut issues, more straightforward debate.

There is a case for such a view. But there is also a case for the contrary attitude. It is possible to argue, with a good deal of force, that the system under which Americans are actually governed, by which both parties have conservative and liberal wings, and by which both seek to gravitate toward the center where the votes are concentrated, breaks the force of extremism and substitutes gradual adaptation and the acceptance of the adaptation for more violent swings of the political pendulum.

But however this may be, whether the President was right or wrong in his objective—he suffered a resounding defeat. Once again, as so often in American politics, it was demonstrated that even a powerful and popular leader (and Roosevelt in 1938 retained immense personal popularity) could not transfer his strength to other candidates. The structure of the traditional parties, it was demonstrated, was not easily to be changed. They were to remain, as they have almost invariably been, loose coalitions of sectional and group interests rather than cohesive organizations with fixed principles. Not even the New Deal years could alter this fact or transform the Democratic party into a party of undiluted liberalism.

The year 1938, as was stated at the beginning of this book, marks a sharp dividing line in the history of the Roosevelt administrations. Some persons would go further and say that it marks the end of the New Deal. To a considerable extent, this position is justified, and it can at least be said that it deserves analysis. What is meant by such an assertion?

First, the whole emphasis changes. After 1938 the important questions are questions of foreign policy. After 1941 the fundamental question is the winning of the war. Second, the legislative policies that characterize the New Deal were virtually all enacted before 1939. The reforming spirit ebbed; the relief problem and the recovery problem both disappeared with the coming of war prosperity. Third, the ascendancy of the Democratic party began to be shaken. In the Congress elected in 1938, as we have seen, the signs of reaction already had appeared. The Republicans gained substantially. In 1940 the Democrats profited from the candidacy of the President and increased their membership to 267. But they went down to 222 in 1942 (a very slender margin) and recovered only to 243 in 1944. In 1946 they lost control. In the Senate the great majorities of 1936 were shrinking also. In 1940 there were 66 Democratic Senators, in 1942 and in 1944 only 57, and in 1946 only 45. Fourth, in the Democratic party itself more and more power was passing to the southern conservatives. Fifth, there was a shift in the position of the workers. It was scarcely to be expected that the great unions would cease to exert substantial influence in politics, and they had become an established feature of the American scene. But the war years made great demands on the energy and high capacity of the leading businessmen of the country, and the attitude of the government was by no means so hostile as it had been when the President denounced the economic royalists in 1936. We must beware of exaggeration. Certainly, antagonism to the Roosevelt administration on the part of the entrepreneurial group did not disappear; certainly the administration itself did not abandon its solicitude for the economic elements having so much to do with its ascendancy. The orientation of the Roosevelt regime was not revolutionized; it was merely modified. But the modification was important. We shall be justified, then, in attempting an assessment of the New Deal at the end of 1938.

The role of the President himself will be stressed by many readers. For many people have a strong inclination to personalize history. In accord with this tendency, Roosevelt was regarded by his admirers as the moving force in the events we have described, as a great political leader who shaped the policies of his time in the interests of the people. He was regarded by others as a sinister politician setting class against class and menacing the foundations

The New Deal Weakens

of the American political and social order. Both these views overestimate the importance of the individual. It is possible to argue that the New Deal had its roots in social circumstance and is more wisely regarded as the reaction of the Americans to the Great Depression rather than as the accomplishment—worthy or unworthy— of any individual. The point can be made clear by recalling the circumstances in which the principal legislative measures of the era were enacted. The agricultural reforms of the New Deal, for example, were related to, if not precisely similar to, the abortive measures proposed (and vetoed) in the administration of Calvin Coolidge. The N.I.R.A. owed its adoption in part to the trade-association movement of the twenties. The devaluation of the dollar in 1934 is reminiscent of the inflationary proposals of 1896, only one in a long line of such measures and not the only one adopted. Use of the Tennessee Valley dams was discussed long before Roosevelt took office. The awakening of labor was in line with the tendencies in every other industrial nation and was, in fact, long overdue in comparison with the experience of Europe. Progressive taxes on the well-to-do were accepted long before 1933. And so might one go on to argue that in dealing with all these measures it was the spirit of the time that dictated action, not simply the will or the intelligence of the Chief Executive.

There is a corollary to this contention. If the legislation of the Roosevelt era sprang from social conditions and had its origins in ways of thought not unknown before 1933, it also follows that the President cannot be given much credit for originality. In the main, it is to be doubted if he would have claimed such a virtue. Perhaps the most personal of all the measures of the period was that creating the Civilian Conservation Corps, a long-time cherished project of Roosevelt before he took office, so his wife assures us. The gold-buying plan would probably not have been tried by a Chief

The New Age of Franklin Roosevelt, 1932–45

Executive more prudent and less experimental by temperament, but its adoption does not suggest profound wisdom. All in all (and this is as it should be) the legislation of the Roosevelt period sprang from many minds in response to deep social demands.

We must again note that in connection with perhaps the most far-reaching change of the period, the new role of labor, the President played a very cautious and "cagey" role. By no stretch of the imagination can he be described as the leader in the fight for the Wagner Act. That title belongs to Senator Wagner himself.

There is still another point to be made. Most of the New Deal measures were passed by huge majorities in both houses of Congress. It is not strange that in the hectic spring of 1933, the period known as the "Hundred Days," this was the case. The country had passed through a grueling experience; it was hungry for positive action, and the action came. But it is more remarkable that the same situation obtained in 1934 and even in 1935. Thus the gold reserve act of 1934 was passed by an overwhelming vote in both the House and the Senate, and it was the same with the Securities Exchange Act and the Emergency Relief Appropriation Act. The Wagner Act passed in the House without a roll call and in the Senate by 63 to 12. The Social Security Act passed the House by 372 to 73 and the Senate by 76 to 6. Moreover, there was substantial Republican support in many cases. This last was not true in the case of the A.A.A. or of the N.I.R.A. in its final form, but the Republican opposition mustered more than half its forces on the negative side only in regard to the Emergency Relief Appropriation Act and the act regulating the utility industry. It is impossible to look at these figures without coming to the conclusion that the New Deal represented the public opinion of the nation.

Yet in stating all these things, it is possible to fall into the contrary error of depersonalizing the events of history. As was said in our opening pages, Roosevelt as an individual bulked large in the events of his epoch. The central reason for this fact lies in the gusto, the optimism, and the feeling for the underdog which he brought to a period of change. Some men cower before alterations of the social order. Some men resent such changes. Some men view them with indifference. Roosevelt viewed them with sympathy and with hope. Coming as he did at the end of a period of immense gloom, he inspired many by his infectious confidence in the future of the country and in the good sense of the American people. There were qualities of deviousness and opportunism in the President, but no one except the most jaundiced could deny the depth of his social sympathies, sympathies movingly expressed as early as the Phi Beta Kappa address delivered at Harvard in 1929. His experimental temper was also in accord with the mood of the country. A grossly superficial but common judgment in the early days of the New Deal was to the effect that at least he was doing something. The country wanted something done.

Furthermore, though it is true that the legislation of the New Deal period was the product of many minds and in line with tendencies that antedated the administration, the President, by his affirmative attitude, had a great deal to do with what occurred. To estimate the place of Roosevelt justly, we must try to imagine what would have occurred if he had placed himself in opposition to the spirit of the time; such an attitude would almost certainly have intensified social unrest, with possibly dangerous consequences. By taking the contrary course, Roosevelt, as is clear beyond peradventure, won the confidence of a large majority of Americans. If he did not lead quite so much as some of his admirers would maintain, at least he *seemed* to be leading.

It cannot justly be said of the President that he was a radical. Radicalism implies a sweeping breach with the existing order. But

The New Age of Franklin Roosevelt, 1932–45

Roosevelt never desired such a breach; it is to such figures as Huey Long and Father Coughlin and Doctor Townsend that we must look for a possibly disruptive view of the problems of the thirties. The President never accepted the headlong plans of the extremists. He had a strong tactical sense; and, though he could on occasion strike out on an independent line, he moved in the main with the great body of opinion. The fantasies of the thirties were not for him; he was experimental rather than revolutionary.

His actual domination of the legislative process has been much exaggerated. His role was highly important at the outset; but by the beginning of his second term he had certainly ceased to control Congress. Indeed, he had disrupted his own party by bringing forward the proposal for the reform of the Supreme Court; and, though he was now and then successful in securing the legislation that he desired, never after that time was he in complete control. This, speaking broadly, is the way things are in the United States. Americans like leadership, but they are rarely blind followers of a leader.

Let us turn from the analysis of the role of the President to the broader questions connected with the New Deal. In the heat of political controversy during the thirties it was frequently stated that the New Deal was a means of destroying the capitalist system. We know now that these judgments were invalid. The American business system has shown unquestionable vitality. In its essence it was not shaken by the reforms of the New Deal. On the contrary, it was to attain sensational success in the years after the war.

What of the contemporary charge that the country was moving into socialism? Socialism is a word that often evokes an emotional rather than a rational response. Essentially, it means the actual operation of the major forms of economic activity by the state. After six years of the New Deal the only important instance in which the government had actually entered into competition with private interests was in the field of electric power. And here it did a job that private industry was at the time apparently not ready to do.

Another charge brought against the New Deal was that it set class against class. That the period of the thirties resulted in a sharpening of class antagonisms is undeniable. The balance of power shifted between business and labor. That this should be accompanied by social tension was inevitable, and that the situation should be exploited by radical elements in our society was no less so. To exercise complete objectivity with regard to such a change was difficult, and few people would contend that Roosevelt attained any such ideal. In the long run, both his political instincts and his social sympathies led him to take sides. But it can hardly be said that disaster ensued. The social fabric was not so ruptured as to weaken the country in the great war effort of the forties. The United States remained—and remains—conspicuous among the great nations of the world as that one in which there is the least class consciousness and the greatest degree of social fluidity. It remains a society in which it is possible to attain great wealth and—within limits—to retain it.

But what of the New Deal measures in a more concrete case? How are they to be judged in the perspective of history? One way of looking at the matter (a way which makes objectivity possible) is to ask the question whether or not they proved to be permanent. Judged by this test, the N.I.R.A. must be regarded as a failure. As has already been said, it was on the way out when the Supreme Court declared it unconstitutional. The President's gold-buying program failed. In a little different category is the administration of relief. One may hope that if the American economy is managed with reasonable wisdom, such drastic measures will not again be necessary. Some of the more ambitious social experiments of the New Deal have not survived the test of time and the swing toward conservatism. The Resettlement Administration was never much of a success; its attempt to deal with the problem of farm tenancy in the South was never carried so far as its sponsors hoped. The CCC died with the period of the war and has not been revived.

A vast amount of the legislation of the period survives, however, and survives unchallenged. No one today thinks of repealing the Social Security Act; indeed, the scope of the act is being extended. No one today would suggest that the banking reforms of the Roosevelt period ought to be repealed or that we should stop regulating the stock exchange and the issuance of securities. Though a later statute has modified the Wagner Act, in part depriving labor of its advantage, the principle of free collective bargaining has not been fundamentally assailed. The control of American staple crops and the subsidization of the farmer are today an accepted basis of policy, though differences in the application of the policy may and do occur. The regulation of maximum hours and minimum wages in industry is now accepted as reasonable and in the social interest; no one proposes the repeal of the statute of 1938.

Even TVA, attacked by its critics as "creeping socialism," has survived the test of time and has a host of defenders in the region where it operates. Though controversy still rages on the usefulness of this enterprise as a yardstick and on the whole question of the desirability of public power as against regulated private power (no one proposes unregulated private power), there are few students of the problem who would not admit that as an enterprise in regional planning the government activities in the valley were impressive and that the existence of the project immensely facilitated the atomic research of the period of the war.

Minor measures in the history of the New Deal might be

The New Deal Weakens

added to those just mentioned, but enough has been said to illustrate the fact that the Roosevelt era left an enormous deposit in the field of American politics and that a large part of its program has become assimilated into the American order.

But there is more to the matter than this. It would be unimaginative, in assessing the positive side of the era, to fail to take account of the relief brought by the Roosevelt administration to many persons suffering from misfortune. The farmers and homeowners who had their mortgages refinanced by the Farm Credit Administration or the Home Owners' Loan Corporation had every reason to be grateful to the government in Washington. Those unemployed, who found themselves the victims of a social situation beyond their control and of poverty that no previous forethought or thrift could have forestalled, felt their self-respect restored by the relief policies of these years. The holders of bank deposits, of savings which they could ill afford to lose, were reassured and protected by the banking legislation of 1933.

Over and above all these matters, there is in the New Deal years the beginning of a changed attitude toward fiscal policy in times of depression which may, in a longer perspective, turn out to be the most significant of all the developments of this eventful period. Down to 1929 the orthodox view of the matter had been to let the economic disease exhaust itself and, while it was doing so, to reduce the expenditures of government and balance the budget at its lowest possible level. But a different theory was propounded in the thirties of which the leading exponent was John Maynard Keynes, already mentioned. The new idea called for massive government expenditures and unbalanced budgets to take up the slack left by the decline in private spending. It would be going much too far to say that the Roosevelt administration resolutely adopted this method. But, on the other hand, the practical policies of the New Deal involved relief for unemployed and distressed citizens, balanced budget or no. These years thus contributed to a less rigid view of the necessity for economy in a depression period than had been held in the past and suggested a new approach to the problem if economic disaster should recur.

It can also be said with some confidence that the New Deal erected some safeguards against an economic reaction as violent as that of 1929. For example, one of the causes of the Great Depression in the United States was the excessive use of credit, particularly in the stock market. The legislation of 1933, 1934, and 1935 made such excessive use less likely, though not, of course, impossible. The social security legislation of the Roosevelt period with its provision for unemployment and old age insurance would operate also to check the economic downswing in a period of decline. The agricultural legislation, by putting a floor under farm prices, might well contribute to stabilization in an economic emergency. None of these things is to be regarded as a total solvent of a very difficult and complex problem, but all of them together seem to make such a catastrophe as 1929 less likely.

Finally, it is arguable that the New Deal period produced a healthier economic order in some other respects. It has been maintained, for example, that, in so far as the program raised the status of farmers and workers, it developed consuming power on a broader basis and thus laid a firmer foundation for the prosperity of industry. Professor Kenneth Galbraith, in a seminal work on the American economy, has argued that it produced forces in some measure countervailing the power of capital and by so doing fortified the economic order as a whole. There is more safety, according to this view, in a balance of power between economic groups than in the domination of any one of them.

However, the multiplication of government offices under the

The New Deal Weakens

New Deal has come under heavy criticism. The absence of a coherent political philosophy and the contradictions in policy of the Roosevelt administration may be unfavorably judged. But the most serious indictment goes much further. It must be categorically asserted that the New Deal did not solve the problem of economic dislocation created by the Depression. It did not bring back prosperity in the full sense of the word; it did not meet the unemployment crisis successfully. One essential to the forward movement of the American economy is new investment. Whatever the reasons (and these probably lie deeper than politics), such new investment, which was on the average of almost $9.5 billion during the years 1925 to 1929 and which disappeared entirely during the Depression, averaged only $1 billion for the period 1933 to 1939 and only $2 billion for the relatively favorable period 1935 to 1939. The number of unemployed which, according to the National Conference Board, was of the order of 14 million when Roosevelt took office, shrank to a low of $4\frac{1}{2}$ million in the summer of 1937, but in each winter in the same period it was about 9 or 10 million. After 1937 the figures again rose, to over 11 million in March, 1938, and remained at 10 million or so until March, 1939. There was a descent again in 1940, but the problem was still a serious one until the war produced a totally new situation and a heavy demand for labor.

The reasons for this failure to grapple effectively with the problems of depression are still a matter of dispute. One school of thought would argue that the operation of the American system depends in no small degree upon the confidence of the business classes in the future. They would say that the encouragement of the entrepreneurial spirit is fundamental to the success of a capitalist order; so, too, is the maintenance of those incentives and rewards that cause that spirit to operate. They would maintain that the New Deal measures, or many of them, tended to check that spirit and so to retard recovery. And they would point to the indubitable fact that it needed World War II to bring the nation out of the economic depths.

Another school of thought would take a different view. It would argue that the social changes of the Depression years were inevitable, the inescapable consequence of the economic disaster itself, and that the administration merely sought to guide a social movement that was, in the circumstances, foreordained. In such circumstances, they would say (pointing to the recovery of the war years for confirmation of their point of view) that only a really bold policy of deficit spending could have set the nation in the direction of recovery.

If one places these two views side by side, it is possible to say that the New Deal fell between two stools. It could not restore business confidence; neither could it launch an audacious and far-reaching program of deficit finance. As a consequence, it failed to solve the fundamental problem of unemployment until the conditions of war placed that problem in a new setting.

It is necessary, therefore, in summary, to understand that the New Deal deserves neither unqualified praise nor unqualified blame. It is best understood as a social process arising out of depression: a social process which altered the political and economic framework without, however, destroying the essential elements of the American system and which introduced many beneficial reforms but which left some problems unsolved.

By 1938, as we have said, the movement had run the greater part of its course, and the years from 1938 to 1945 are concerned primarily with questions of foreign policy. It is to the origin and evolution of these questions that we must now turn.

I V

The Good Neighbor and the Reluctant World Power

There have been periods in the history of the United States when foreign policy occupied a subordinate place, but the age of Roosevelt was not one of them. Withdrawal or participation—that was the choice confronting the American people. They began by wishing to evade all responsibility for the world outside their borders. They ended by accepting responsibility as a major world power. The America of 1933 turned in on itself. The America of 1945 could not divest itself of world-wide interests. The story of this change is central and fundamental to an understanding of the times.

We begin with what has been called American isolationism, and at the outset we must underline a fact not sufficiently stressed by historians. The scholar is tempted to think in terms of rational behavior, to seek "the causes" of action, national or international, in some intellectual pattern of conduct clearly comprehended and resolutely acted upon. Of course every policy, every decision in politics, has its rationalization. But behind the conduct of nations, as behind the conduct of individuals, lies an emotional state, which, as a rule, transcends the logical processes by which it is justified. To put the matter another way, the mood of a nation is often as important as its opinions; public sentiment is often as important as public judgment.

There were many reasons why the United States should be isolationist in 1933. The Great Depression itself was the best of all reasons. Confronting the most serious problems of internal adjustment that they had ever faced, the American people were reluctant to project their gaze beyond the seas. It was the easier to ignore overseas events because, of all the great nations, America had the most naïve view of the role of force in international affairs. The nation had risen to greatness without engaging in large-scale war, and "power politics" in the European sense had played very little part in the process. Without experience in this field, Americans viewed the competitions of Europe as a sinister game which they neither desired nor felt compelled to play. Moreover, the experience of intervention in World War I had not been a particularly enheartening one. The generation most influential politically in the thirties had seen the idealistic program of Woodrow Wilson roughly handled at Paris; it had seen selfishness supplant altruism; and it had seen, just as President Roosevelt entered office, the nations of the Old World repudiate their indebtedness to the United States. Had Americans crossed the seas in 1917 and 1918, given money and blood for the relief of Europe from German oppression, only to come to this result? The complaint could be, and was, pushed further. Since scapegoats are always useful in this world, it was easy to believe, as President Hoover believed, that America would have emerged much sooner from the depression if it had not been for the European economic crisis of 1931, if the wrangling nations of the Old World had not deepened their own economic difficulties by political rivalries, if they had not intensified their own misery by folly and the game of power. And, on top of all this, there subsisted, as there still subsists today, the notion that there is something unique about the political and economic order of the United States and that only contamination could come from closer association with the wicked world outside American borders.

Views such as these were current throughout the thirties. They found perhaps their most cogent intellectual expression in one of the most respected, and one of the most read, American historians, Charles A. Beard, who, in the course of the decade, expounded at length the theory of an America living in its own hemisphere, developing its own resources, and carefully abstaining from participation in world politics. There were others who took the same line, for example, Stuart Chase, an author with a marvelous gift for (sometimes misleading) simplification, and Oswald Garrison Villard, the courageous if somewhat confused editor of *The Nation*. The same temper was reflected in American literature. When Ernest Hemingway wrote *A Farewell to Arms* in 1929, he emphasized the futility of war; Robert Sherwood, who must later have repented, embroidered the same theme in *The Idiot's Delight*; and John Dos Passos in *U.S.A.* gave currency to the doctrine of disillusionment. The temper of the times was reflected in all these men; and it was the temper of the times that determined the attitude of the Roosevelt administration.

When Franklin Roosevelt took the oath of office for the first time, the international scene was by no means a cheerful one. In Germany, only a few weeks before Roosevelt's inauguration, a sinister and powerful demagogue had reaped the fruits of his long agitation and become the Chancellor of the German Reich. Adolf Hitler, to be sure, spoke fair words at the beginning; but it was not long before he swept away the democratic constitution of Weimar and vested himself with a power as terrible as it was to be complete. His rise to authority reflected the surcharged nationalism of the German people, their discontent with the treaty of Versailles, and their reaction to the Depression. In the eyes of the most discerning, it boded nothing but ill for the future. At the same time, on the other side of the world, the tide of Japanese militarism was steadily mounting. In the fall of 1931 the Japanese had occupied all of Manchuria. The attempts of the League of Nations and the attempt of the Hoover administration operating in conjunction with the League failed to persuade them to desist, and, when a League commission rendered its report on the Manchurian question, a report highly critical of Japanese action, the Japanese had walked out of the League Assembly in Geneva. This was only a few days before the Roosevelt inauguration.

But in the mood of 1933 it was easy for the American people to avert their gaze from these events, and it is not strange, therefore, that the best efforts of Roosevelt's first term in the field of foreign policy were exerted in the field of Latin-American diplomacy. Here the task was simpler than in Europe or in Asia; here the reaction against the wicked world across the two great oceans facilitated a return to a hemispheric diplomacy; here the way had been in some measure prepared by the previous administration. The policy of the "good neighbor," as it was to be called, though owing much to Roosevelt and Secretary of State Cordell Hull, had already been adumbrated by the course of Herbert Hoover and Henry L. Stimson.

Of all the great nations of the world, the United States least deserves to be described by the term "imperialistic." True, at the turn of the century, somewhat in the spirit of "keeping up with the Joneses" the American people had embarked upon a policy of colonial acquisition. True, in the years that followed, the government had at one time or another sent American marines to police the more turbulent and disorderly countries of the Caribbean. Between 1898 and 1921 American policy justified intervention in the

The Good Neighbor and the Reluctant World Power

affairs of other states in the New World on the familiar ground that such action was necessary to prevent intervention by others and with the avowed purpose of reforming the political morale of the inhabitants of the republics in question But even at its apogee, American imperialism was imperialism with an uneasy conscience; and the reaction against it had already begun in the twenties and had attained considerable momentum when the Democratic administration came into power.

In his inaugural address President Roosevelt had defined his foreign policy as the policy of the "good neighbor." The phrase was meant to have a universal and not a restricted geographical application, but it was so pat a description of his course of action in the Western Hemisphere that it soon became closely identified with that area. Here, as in other matters, Roosevelt sensed the public mood and translated it into action.

In his policy toward Latin America Roosevelt was much assisted by his two principal aides in the field of foreign affairs. Cordell Hull, the Secretary of State from 1933 to 1944, was precisely the kind of man to become enthusiastic over the goodneighbor policy. There have been few secretaries of state so prone to think in abstract principles, so attached to broad formulas of action, so persistent in expressing American policy in terms of aspirations and ideals. Possibly this was so because his grasp of facts and his experience were limited when he came to office. Moreover, Hull had been a devoted follower of Woodrow Wilson. Despite Wilson's lapses from idealism in his dealings with the republics to the south, the spirit of his diplomacy had often reflected that regard for the rights of other states which was to become an essential element in the diplomacy of the new administration. Hull found in his memories of the past a strong support for the policies which he was to put into action.

But another figure strongly influenced the development of United

States relations with Latin America. Sumner Welles, the Under-Secretary of State, had been, long before 1933, a sturdy opponent of the interventions in the Caribbean. At a time when interest in Latin-American affairs was at a somewhat low ebb among professional diplomats, he had made a specialty of these matters and had been chief of the Latin-American Affairs Division of the Department of State in 1921-22. He had gone to the same private school as the President, and to the same university as well. More sophisticated than Hull, closer to Roosevelt personally, ambitious and vigorous, he was a person to be reckoned with even at the outset, when he was only an assistant secretary. And though he and Hull were frequently to be at swords' points in the ten years of their association, though the President's habit of bypassing the Secretary of State was to introduce a painful element into the relations of Hull and Welles, each supplemented the other in our dealings with the republics to the south. Welles knew much more than Hull; but Hull, as a veteran politician and a former congressman and senator, was better qualified to translate the policy of the administration into terms that could be understood and appreciated on Capitol Hill.

There were many respects in which the times especially favored the good-neighbor concept. The danger of European intervention in the New World, the avowed justification of the interventions of the earlier era, seemed still remote in 1933. The Latin-American states had made plain their profound resentment at the meddling of the United States in their affairs. Many Americans believed (erroneously) that our Caribbean policy had been framed in the interests of the bankers, and bankers were not at the height of their popularity in 1933. American commercial interests hoped to benefit by a policy of good will. The administration had little to lose by the wooing of the republics to the south. Furthermore, in a long perspective (though this may not have been perceived at the time), the friendship of Latin America might be of substantial advantage if war broke out in Europe.

What was the essence of the good-neighbor policy? The root principle was the principle of non-interference in the affairs of independent states. It would, however, have been one thing to enunciate this principle in general terms; it was an entirely different matter to incorporate it in a formal diplomatic document. The Latin-American states had clamored for such a commitment at the Pan-American conference at Havana in 1928; and it had needed all the lawyer-like ability and diplomatic skill of Charles Evans Hughes to stave off action. But at the conference of Montevideo in 1933 and again at Buenos Aires in 1936, Secretary Hull gave them what they asked for. His manners and methods in dealing with the sometimes sticky pride of Latin-American diplomats were widely applauded; even the vainest of foreign ministers, Saavedra Lamas of Argentina, succumbed to his homely charm; and at home the Secretary had the satisfaction of seeing the agreements that he signed ratified unanimously by the Senate. Moreover, the United States gave early proof of its sincerity. In spite of great temptation, on account of the large American interests involved, it made no move toward intervention when a somewhat radical regime arose in Cuba; and, in 1934, when that regime was succeeded by a more conservative one, the United States agreed to the abrogation of the Platt amendment by which, as far back as 1901, it had reserved the right to intervene in the affairs of the island. In 1934 came the evacuation of Haiti and the departure of the last of the marines from the soil of any independent state. In 1936 an agreement with Panama ended American tutelage of that republic.

A second principle of the good-neighbor policy was inter-American co-operation. At Buenos Aires the nations of the New World

(Argentina reluctantly consenting) agreed to consult together in the event of an international war "which might menace the peace of the American hemisphere." Two years later machinery was provided to carry this pledge into effect, and on this second occasion, at Lima, a resounding declaration of American principles was adopted.

A third aspect of the good-neighbor policy was the lowering of trade barriers. This was a favorite idea of Secretary Hull. Unsuccessful in imposing it on the President in 1933, Hull continued to press for action, and the result was the reciprocal trade agreement act of 1934 which authorized a 50 per cent reduction of tariff duties by presidential action in understandings with other states. To such a country as Cuba, heavily dependent on the American market, this was a decided boon.

Finally, the good-neighbor policy was characterized by a remarkable tolerance toward the economic policies of the Latin-American republics. The administration stood aloof from the controversies raised by the defaults of many of these republics on their debts, and it pursued a most restrained policy when they handled American interests roughly. When, for example, the Bolivian government expropriated the holdings of the Standard Oil Company in Bolivia, the State Department raised no great protest. And when, in a measure much more far-reaching in effect, the Mexican government followed the same course, no particular outcry came from Washington, though a very limited settlement of American claims was made in 1940. When America entered the war in 1941, it was to reap its rewards in the remarkable solidarity of the American states.

The successes of American policy toward Latin America were hardly matched either in Asia or in Europe. In our outstanding controversy with Japan the President could hardly retreat from the position assumed by his predecessor, namely, that the United States would not recognize the new situation created by the Japanese occupation of Manchuria. But neither could he take positive action of any kind. The country was in no mood for a policy of adventure, and Roosevelt reflected the mood. Indeed, he may well have thought at the beginning of his term that he might let the controversy with Japan gradually fade away. Secure in its knowledge that America would not act, Tokyo proceeded from one aggressive step to another. In the spring of 1934 a spokesman of the Japanese foreign office declared that Japan had special interests in China and warned the Western powers against any action prejudicial to those interests. In the latter part of the same year the Japanese government denounced the treaties of naval limitation which had been signed in 1922 and 1930, for a time putting a stop to the competition in armaments in the Orient. In 1935 the five northern provinces of China were brought under the direct influence of Japan and erected into an "autonomous area." In 1936, when a conference was held at London to try to work out new naval arrangements, the Japanese made it clear that they would insist upon equality with the United States. Since the earlier agreements had established a ratio of 5 to 3, the American government could do nothing but refuse to accept any such proposal, and when this became clear, the Japanese simply bolted. In the summer of 1937 Tokyo began what it preferred to describe mellifluously as "the China incident" but what was in fact the actual waging of war against the Chinese republic. In the fall of that year an American vessel of war in the Yangtze river was wantonly bombed by Japanese aviators. And during all this period American trade in Manchuria was hampered and American interests inconsiderately handled.

The temper of American opinion with regard to the Far East

in these years was shown by the strong desire manifested in Congress to get out of the Philippines. It was in consonance with American promises and American ideals that the islands should some day receive their independence, but the movement in this direction in the thirties was motivated by no such lofty conceptions. A combination of interests, especially the beet-sugar interests, which suffered from Filipino competition, and of isolationists who hoped for an abdication of responsibility in the Far East was responsible for the bill that passed Congress in 1934. In the course of the debate the argument was frequently used that the islands represented a dangerous commitment on which the American taxpayer would never be willing to make good. The independence measure provided for the withdrawal of the United States from its military bases at the end of ten years and left for future discussion the question of naval bases. In the meantime Congress neglected the defenses of Guam, the island outpost in the Pacific.

The administration by no means entirely consented to the course of events in the Orient. Hull, according to his custom, addressed numerous moral homilies to the Japanese government, which, however eloquent, changed not a tittle the actual posture of affairs. The President sought ever larger and larger appropriations for the navy, and by 1936/37 and 1937/38 these had become the greatest in history. In the fall of 1937, moreover, he sought to arouse American opinion. Speaking in the Middle West, in the midst of the region most isolationist in sentiment, he declared that "peace-loving nations" must "make a concerted effort in opposition to those violations of treaties and those ignorings of humane instincts which are today creating a state of international anarchy and instability from which there is no escape through mere isolation or neutrality." War, he went on to argue, must be quarantined like an epidemic disease. But it is no exaggeration to say that the speech fell flat, and the President himself seemed to skate away from any concrete application of his formula when press correspondents sought to elicit further information as to his intentions. Though Secretary Hull issued a statement shortly afterward that the policy of the Japanese government was "inconsistent with the principles which should govern the relationship between nations, and with the principle of the Nine-Power treaty guaranteeing the integrity of China," though he indorsed the findings of a League committee as to Japanese aggression and accepted an invitation extended by the Belgian government to a conference at Brussels to discuss the situation in the Far East, no one of these steps altered in any essential way the existing situation or roused American opinion to demand effective action against Japan. On the contrary, the whole tide of public sentiment was flowing rapidly and, as it seemed, conclusively in favor of a policy of caution.

If it was not easy to rouse the American public where flagrant aggression had already taken place and where the interests of the United States were clearly menaced, it is not surprising that the Roosevelt administration made no great effort to shape its European policy along lines of co-operative effort. Both in the field of armaments and in the field of economic policy, the President and his advisers were powerless to check the ominous course of events.

In the matter of armaments the situation was this. For some time Germany, disarmed by the treaty of Versailles, had been clamoring for the lifting of the restrictions on its armed forces. A conference had been convened in 1932 and was again in session in the spring of 1933. The French, justly suspicious of the great power across the Rhine, and especially of the new Reich of Adolf Hitler, wished some kind of guaranty against aggression in exchange for a grant of permission to the Germans to expand their military establishment. But such a guaranty was impossible for the United States to give. The utmost that the President could do was to declare, through his special representative Norman Davis, that in case the League of Nations applied sanctions against Germany, the United States would not interfere with such sanctions. Such a statement was pitifully inadequate to meet the situation. When, shortly after the Roosevelt offer, Germany abandoned the conference and a few months later withdrew from the League, it was clear that a new period of arms competition was at hand. The most farsighted observers already saw the dangers in the path ahead.

The international economic situation in the spring of 1933 was as complex and as filled with pitfalls as was the arms problem. In 1931 Great Britain had gone off gold, that is, had declined any longer to measure its currency in terms of a fixed amount of the precious metal, and had permitted the value of its monetary unit to be fixed by the demand for pounds in international trade. Its example was followed by other nations, and a currency war resulted. In order to put an end to these conditions, much resented in the United States since devaluation permitted the British to sell their products more cheaply abroad, the previous administration had accepted an invitation to an international conference to be held in London. The commitment was honored by the new regime, and initially the language of the Chief Executive suggested strong sympathy with these objectives. On May 7, 1933, in his second fireside chat, Roosevelt declared that the United States was seeking a cutting-down of trade barriers and "the setting up of a stabilization of currencies." On May 16 he issued an "Appeal to the Nations," in which he again indorsed the purposes of the projected conference.

But he did not long remain faithful to these pronouncements. The delegation that he sent to London was principally distinguished for the division of views among its members and for the limited knowledge possessed by them with regard to the complex problems to be discussed. Secretary Hull, the chairman, was not even consulted about the choice of his colleagues. He himself clung with his usual tenacity to the idea of tariff reductions, but he possessed no expert knowledge of currency matters. And, even on the tariff, he was undercut at home by his Assistant Secretary of State, Raymond Moley, one of Roosevelt's original braintrusters, who made no bones about minimizing the importance of international trade. As prices began to rise at home, in other words as the dollar fell in value, the President became less and less anxious to tie himself up to any scheme of stabilization. The protectionist sentiment in Congress, stronger in 1933 than it was to be a year later, also diminished his enthusiasm for any projects for lowering duties. As the conference proceeded, his attitude became more and more unco-operative. He rejected a "temporary" stabilization agreement negotiated with the British and French, and a little later he turned down a new and vague arrangement proposed by Moley, who had been sent to London as the President's special emissary, which looked to an eventual return to the gold standard. Finally, in a message of July 3, a message that almost reduced Secretary Hull to despair, Roosevelt came near to disrupting the conference by rejecting in strong terms any idea of stabilized currencies and by reading his European friends a lecture on the necessity of balanced budgets, raising of the price level, and domestic reforms. Although the conference staggered on for a few weeks, it adjourned without substantial accomplishment.

The message from the "Indianapolis" was an example of economic nationalism. Moreover, in the long run, stabilized currencies and lower tariffs were to prove in the interest of the United States. But it is only fair to say that in the context of the spring of 1933 it is by no means certain that the President was wrong. By cheapening the pound in 1931 the British had gained an advantage over the United States in the field of international trade. In order to reduce this advantage it was necessary to let the dollar itself fall in value, and by the early summer of 1933 it was not easy to be sure that the fall had been sufficient to justify a new stabilization agreement. At any rate, the President was at that time wedded to a course of action utterly incompatible with the success of the conference, and there is little evidence that his action met with much condemnation from American public opinion. The fact is that in 1933 and in the years that followed (as we have already said) a large proportion of the American people looked upon any association with Europe, political or economic, with a jaundiced eye.

One of the manifestations of this attitude (and one of the most remarkable) was the movement to discredit the policies of Woodrow Wilson and to look upon the events of the years 1917–18 as an example, not of wisdom, but of folly. This movement has been described by the professional historians as "revisionism." It has been characteristic of Americans to regret war after it has happened. This reaction is no doubt due to a number of factors. It has its deepest significance, perhaps, as an indication of the strongly pacific strain in the national character. It derives some of its force from the difficulty the ordinary man experiences in time of peace in understanding the passion which others, or even he himself, felt at another epoch and in other circumstances. It is buttressed oftentimes by the desire of partisans to denigrate the leader in the war period if he belonged to the opposite political sect. It is reinforced by the disillusionment almost invariably following on armed conflict when it is discovered that, far from solving every problem, war creates new problems of its own. And, finally, in this particular case it derived some of its force from the intense and natural preoccupation of the American people with their own internal affairs in the first Roosevelt administration.

Only a few years after the treaty of Versailles, John Kenneth Turner expressed the revisionist view in a virulent book, *Shall It Be Again?* The researches of Professor Sidney B. Fay and the more passionate and biased investigations of Harry Elmer Barnes, though they dealt with the responsibility of the various European nations for the war of 1914–18, by shaking the orthodox view that the whole blame lay with Germany, no doubt contributed to a new set of opinion. In 1929 C. Hartley Grattan in *Why We Fought* suggested, without affirming, that the American cause in 1917 had not been quite so free of sordid elements as Americans might like to believe. And in 1935, with a book whose literary brilliance did much to win men to its view, Walter Millis in *The Road to War* expressed in persuasive form the thesis that America had muddled into the conflict with Germany rather than entered it with clear aims and high purposes.

In the meantime another development had taken place. In March, 1934, the magazine *Fortune* published a sensational article on the armaments business. Most of what it had to say concerned the tie-up between European arms manufacturers and politicians, often an unpleasant story. But the activity of the American steel companies at the Geneva naval conference of 1927 was also recalled. Hard on the appearance of this article the Senate voted to investigate the arms traffic. By a curious mental operation on the part of Senator Pittman, who was the chairman of the Foreign Affairs Committee, Senator Nye of North Dakota, a Republican of distinctly isolationist slant, was chosen to direct the inquiry. The chief investigator and informal counsel for the committee was Stephen Raushenbush, and under his spur the investigation went far beyond its original purpose. The policies of the Woodrow Wilson administration were sharply criticized, and the thesis that American entry into the war was the work of wicked Wall Street bankers, aided and abetted by sinister arms barons, gained headway accordingly with American public opinion. The thesis, it is worthwhile to remark, was unsound. It was then—and is now—impossible to prove that these influences determined the course of President Wilson. Indeed, he was deeply reluctant to enter the war, and it is difficult to believe that, had the Germans not renewed the submarine campaign (temporarily suspended) in the winter of 1917, he could have been brought to such action. But in public affairs it is not the accuracy but the force of a belief that counts, and there can be little doubt that the tide was running strongly toward revisionism in 1934 and 1935.

In such circumstances Congress reacted in vigorous fashion to the drift of public opinion. Cordell Hull, with his Wilsonian background, was by no means enthusiastic about what began to be called "neutrality legislation," but President Roosevelt, opportunist politician that he often was, made no attempt to stem the developing movement. The first discussions turned on an embargo against the munitions traffic in time of war. Such an embargo, framed in absolute terms, was sure to benefit the most heavily armed and therefore, in all probability, the aggressor nation, and it would run squarely athwart any coercive action by the League of Nations against a law-breaking state. In the House these considerations had weight, and the imposition of the embargo was left to the discretion of the President, but the Senate took the bit in its teeth, and, in its final form, the arms legislation left no choice to the executive but to apply the prohibition on arms export to all nations at war without distinction. The President, aware of the strength of congressional feeling, signed the law with a commentary on its provisions and the expression of a hope that "more permanent legislation might provide for greater flexibility." He was later very much to regret his action.

The temper of Congress in the session of 1935 was demonstrated in another fashion. For a period of more than a decade the question of American adhesion to the protocol setting up the World Court had been much discussed. Nothing could have been more innocent than this proposal; for the court was a court of voluntary jurisdiction, and action on the protocol did not bind the United States to submit any specific question whatsoever to the international tribunal. Yet, from its first appearance in 1923, the court issue seemed to rouse substantial opposition. The court judges were elected by League machinery, and to the foes of the League, including such powerful senators as Borah, this alone was enough to condemn the whole idea. In 1926 the Senate had ratified the protocol but with reservations that proved distasteful to the many nations who had accepted the court. Painful negotiation followed on the reservations, and, when accord was reached, long delay followed on that accord. It was not until the spring of 1935 that the new agreement came before the Senate for ratification. And then occurred a most astounding phenomenon. A flood of protests swept into Washington, spearheaded by the nationalistic publisher William Randolph Hearst and by Father Coughlin, who, as we have seen, then enjoyed wide radio popularity. Some 200,000 telegrams came to senators in a few days—40,000 in a single day—all of them expressing bitter opposition to the court. In the face of such a demonstration the Senate capitulated. The protocol failed of ratification by a vote of 52 to 36. Very rarely has a vote been accompanied by so much unreason.

Throughout the debate on the court the President had maintained an indifferent attitude. He had no mind to breast the tide of sentiment; the vote on the subject only confirmed the administration in its extremely cautious attitude with regard to the whole problem of neutrality. This circumspection was soon to be demonstrated in a matter of far greater significance.

The League of Nations had been powerless to check the aggression of Japan. In 1935 and 1936 it was to be put to a new test. The Italian dictator Benito Mussolini had for some time coveted Ethiopia. The Italians had attempted the conquest of that kingdom as far back as 1895 and had been humiliatingly defeated at the battle of Adowa. Thus the desire for revenge reinforced the acquisitive instincts of the Fascist chieftain. Trouble began to brew in the latter part of 1934 when a border clash was followed by a demand for reparations on the part of the Ethiopian government. In October, 1935, after futile efforts at negotiation, the war began. Five days after the Italian troops crossed the frontier, the League Council found by a unanimous vote that Italy had violated the Covenant and committed an act of aggression. On November 18 the members of the League, acting with extraordinary accord, declared an arms embargo, an embargo on credits, a ban on Italian imports, and a partial ban on exports. But there was a serious weakness in its operations. The most vital of all exports to Italy was oil. And this the Italians were allowed to continue to buy from the outside world. Moreover, in the face of threat of war, the League leaders began to take fright. In December the French and British foreign ministers brought forward a proposal that was in effect a partial capitulation and the purchase of Italian good will. The public reaction was strong, especially in Great Britain; and Sir Samuel Hoare, the architect of this proposal, was driven from office. But the League never did muster its courage to carry through a decisive program, and in due course the movement for sanctions collapsed. The Emperor of Ethiopia, the unfortunate Haile Selassie, was compelled to bow before the power of the new Rome.

The Good Neighbor and the Reluctant World Power

What was the attitude of the Roosevelt administration during the course of these events? It is fair to say that it was less cooperative, so far as the League was concerned, than the attitude of Secretary Stimson in 1931. "With the isolationist sentiment so strong," says Secretary Hull in his memoirs, "it was impossible to join any League body considering sanctions. I preferred that any action we took should be entirely independent and not even seem to be suggested by the League." This attitude was maintained throughout the whole Ethiopian imbroglio, and it was approved by the President himself. On the other hand, there were signs that, within certain sharply defined political limits, there was a disposition to assist the Geneva organization. Thus, shortly after the application of an arms embargo on both belligerents (a step dictated by previous legislation), Secretary Hull issued a public statement declaring that "the American people are entitled to know that there are certain commodities such as oil, copper, trucks, scrap iron and scrap steel which are essential war materials, although not actually 'arms, ammunition or implements of war,' and that according to recent trade reports, a considerably increased amount of these is being exported for war purposes. This class of trade is directly contrary to the policy of this Government as announced in official statements of the President and Secretary of State, as it is also contrary to the general spirit of the recent Neutrality Act." But this moral embargo, if it may so be called, had very little effect. A little later the British ambassador asked what would be the position of the United States if the League powers declared an oil embargo. In reply to this inquiry Hull entirely declined to commit himself but suggested that the League members "cease their backing and filling and take a resolute course" without waiting for the United States. Though he was apparently turning over in the back of his mind the idea of limiting oil exports from the United States to normal prewar quantities, he would give no assurances whatsoever. And it is probably true that, had he sought to secure from Congress new legislation limiting Italian trade, he would have failed in his objective.

We must not imagine that the action of the United States was the crucial factor in the collapse of sanctions. It was the weakness and irresolution of European statesmen, not the attitude of Washington, that was decisive. The Ethiopian question demonstrated the immense difficulties in the way of economic sanctions as a substitute for war. Mussolini had threatened to fight if oil was embargoed, and the threat was sufficient to prevent action. No European power was ready to make the ultimate sacrifice for the benefit of Haile Selassie. The only beneficiary of the League action was Hitler, who took advantage of the confused situation to occupy the hitherto demilitarized Rhineland and thus to move one step further toward the consolidation of his power.

In the United States the breakdown of sanctions confirmed the isolationists in their point of view. Congress, pressing forward along the path already marked out, in 1936 enacted further neutrality legislation which, in addition to its embargo provisions, forbade the extending of loans to belligerents. When civil war broke out in Spain in the summer of 1936, the same formula was applied. The prevailing philosophy that the way to avoid war was to refuse to assist either of the belligerents was futile and even dangerous. In the case of an international war, as we have said, it would mean strengthening the aggressor against his victim, and in a civil war it tended to encourage revolt against an established government by denying arms to constituted authority. But the majorities in favor of this course were overwhelming, and the President hesitated to put his prestige to the test by vetoing such legislation.

The tide of sentiment represented by the Neutrality Acts did not cease to flow in 1936, but in 1937 and 1938 there were some signs, though only slight, of a reaction. When the national legislature set about framing a permanent statute in the first of these years, conflicting points of view were evident. Apart from the fact that the restriction on trade militated against a victim of aggression, there was the fact that commerce in time of war might be of great benefit to the United States and that to cut it off entirely might work serious damage to the national economy. A certain ambivalence was evident in the action of Congress. In pursuance of its objective of preventing (on the basis of American experience in the last war) involvement in the next one, the new legislation made it mandatory for the President to warn Americans off belligerent merchant ships. But with regard to trade, it was finally decided that the middle course was to permit belligerents to buy in the American market, provided that they paid in cash and carried away their purchases in their own vessels. The list of commodities to which this provision was to apply was to be fixed by the President himself.

There was to be a final expression of the isolationist philosophy in 1938. The most extraordinary of all proposals of this extraordinary epoch is what came to be known as the Ludlow amendment to the Constitution. This amendment, introduced by an Indiana congressman, provided that the United States could enter a war only after a national referendum. The American people, faced perhaps by some instant danger, were supposed to debate the issue in every part of the land, expose their divisions to the possible enemy, and fracture their national unity in time of peril by sharp and perhaps bitter discussion. Moreover, if such a measure were not dangerous, it would prove to be futile. For as the history of the United States demonstrates, the actual declaration of war usually follows protracted negotiation which, under our constitutional forms, is in the hands of the President. Wars do not come about suddenly. A long train of events makes up the issues on which the final decision depends. A wise President will be guided by public opinion in determining these issues, but the nation will doubtless in the future, as in the past, wish to sustain the Chief Executive.

Nevertheless, the idea contained in the Ludlow amendment had much support. A public opinion poll showed that 75 per cent of those questioned were in favor of the principle in 1935, 68 per cent in 1938. When the issue was brought to the floor of the House in the latter year, it was clear that a great parliamentary battle impended. The President spoke out against the proposal; so, too, did the Secretary of State. When the vote was taken, the count stood 209 in the affirmative and 188 in the negative (a two-thirds vote being required). Three out of every four Republicans had been recorded as in favor of this remarkable measure, and three out of every eight Democrats had taken the same position.

The Ludlow amendment represents the isolationist sentiment in its most extreme form. It was based on distrust of the executive, on a conception of foreign policy which would have accentuated internal division and made effective action impossible, on that kind of fear of war which encourages others to war. It was the high-water mark of the movement of American withdrawal. But before many months had gone by, the scene shifted drastically, and a new era arrived. Events in Europe set the stage for great changes in the orientation of American diplomacy.

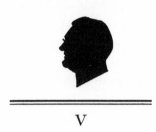

V

The Deepening Crisis

By 1938 American isolationism had reached its full flower. If we are disposed to judge it harshly, in view of what transpired later, it is well to remember that not only was it the natural product of a period of intense preoccupation with domestic affairs but that it was closely paralleled by the behavior of the European democracies. France and Great Britain, no less than the United States, suffered during these years from a kind of paralysis in the international field and from a strong disinclination to take any positive action to arrest the growth of totalitarianism. They, no less than the United States, were indifferent to the advance of the Japanese. They, no more than the United States—and perhaps with more at stake—made no effective move to interfere with the Italian conquest of Ethiopia. They saw Hitler leave the League of Nations; they saw him tear up the disarmament clauses of the treaty of Versailles; they saw him build up his forces for aggression while still professing peace; they saw him enter the demilitarized Rhineland; and in 1938 they saw his forces conquer Austria. The tide of violence still mounted. Under threat of war Hitler in the fall of 1938 demanded from Czechoslovakia the cession of the so-called Sudetenland (largely inhabited by Germans). The great powers, far from resisting, brought pressure to bear on the Czechoslovak government to yield, and the result was what its critics called the capitulation at Munich. Before many months had passed, a new act of violence occurred. Violating his solemn promises, Hitler repudiated the agreement just made and in March, 1939, strode up the steps of the castle of the Hradschin in Prague and proclaimed the extinction of the Czechoslovak state. Only with this latter act were the European democracies galvanized into action, extending guaranties to Poland (clearly the next probable victim of Hitlerian aggression) and entering into anti-German negotiations with the Soviet Union.

The change that came in Europe in 1939, the growing sense of the necessity of taking a stand against further aggression, had by no means at this time taken place in the United States. We shall soon have occasion to trace the evolution of American opinion in detail. But we should begin by some generalizations. First of all, there did exist, even in the middle thirties, a strong moral opprobrium in America with regard to wars of conquest. It was public sentiment that had demanded, back as far as 1928, the negotiation of the Kellogg-Briand pact, which bound the nations of the world not to resort to war as the instrument of national policy. Public sentiment condemned, even in the midst of its preoccupation with home affairs, the aggressions of Japan. Public sentiment reacted against the excesses of Hitler and particularly against the Munich conference. Even so strong a pacifist as Oswald Garrison Villard was shocked, though, like other pacifists, he could not draw from his own moral revulsion the necessary conclusion that it was sometimes necessary to be ready to fight in order to ward off evil. If these feelings had little influence on policy, the reason is not far to seek: the American people did not as yet feel insecure. It was when fear was added to moral condemnation that their temper began to change and that in increasing measure they began to feel that they might be compelled, in their own interest, to combat the advance of totalitarianism.

The European crisis of the fall of 1938 produced no important declaration of policy on the part of the administration. In November, when the chronic anti-Semitism of the Hitler regime resulted in a particularly outrageous outbreak of violence against the Jews, the President did, indeed, call the American ambassador home from Germany for "consultation" (a manifestation of displeasure). But the clear sign of a new orientation came with the speech that Roosevelt delivered to Congress at the beginning of 1939, sounding the call of danger for all to hear.

"There comes a time," he declared, "in the affairs of men when they must prepare to defend not their homes alone, but the tenets of faith and humanity on which their churches, their government and their very civilization are founded. We know what might happen to us if the new philosophy of force were to encompass the other continents and invade our own. We, no more than other nations, can afford to be surrounded by the enemies of our faith and our humanity. The world has grown so small and weapons of attack so swift that no nation can be safe in its will to pursue peace so long as any other single nation refuses to settle its grievances at the council table. . . . In our foreign relations we have learned from the past what not to do. From new wars we have learned what we must do. We have learned that effective timing of defense and the distant points from which attacks may be launched are completely different from what they were twenty years ago. We have learned that survival cannot be guaranteed after the attack begins—for there is a new speed and range to offense. We have learned that before any overt military act aggression begins with preliminaries of propaganda, subsidized penetration, the loosening of ties of good will, the stirring of prejudice and the incitement to disunion."

Nor did the President confine himself to mere generalities. He recommended the stepping-up of defense appropriations and expressed the opinion that the neutrality legislation of 1937 might operate unevenly, might "actually give aid to an aggressor and deny it to the victim"—a hint, looking to the repeal of the embargo on the arms traffic that had been incorporated in the statute of less than two years before.

In March, 1939, as already indicated, Hitler entered Prague and entirely suppressed the Czech state. In April, in feeble imitation of the German dictator, Mussolini invaded Albania. Roosevelt addressed a long appeal to the two tyrants urging that they give assurances of their peaceable intentions to some thirty nations mentioned by name; and he indicated that if such pledges of non-aggression were received, he would seek similar pledges from each of the nations concerned. From Italy he received no answer whatsoever. From the Fuehrer came a brilliantly deceptive speech that turned the edge of the President's proposals, denying that any ambitious enterprises were afoot and declaring that Germany's neighbors had themselves assured the Reich (as how could they decline to do?) that they felt quite comfortable in the presence of German armament. Roosevelt appeared for the moment to be checkmated; yet it may be that his action gave pause to the Axis powers and that it was not without effect upon the development of American opinion.

By July Hitler had begun a diplomatic campaign against Poland. In view of the commitments made by Great Britain and France, it was becoming clear that German demands against the Poles would lead to a general war.

In January, as we have just seen, the President had hinted at the desirability of repealing the arms embargo. He now stepped up the pressure, and in July a conference was held with congressional leaders to discuss the matter. But these men were not convinced. Senator Borah of Idaho, faithful to the isolationist creed that he had professed ever since the fight on the treaty of Versailles, strongly opposed action and even had the effrontery to tell Secretary Hull that he (Borah) had sources of information superior to those of the Department of State and that there would be no war. The Democratic leaders were not so complacent; but Vice-President Garner assured the President that the votes could not be found for repeal. On August 24, repeating his tactics of September, 1938, Roosevelt appealed to Hitler, to Mussolini, and to President Moscicki of Poland to bend their utmost efforts to the avoidance of war; and, receiving a favorable reply from Moscicki, he next day sent a special appeal to the Fuehrer. But there was, after all, no will to peace in Berlin. On September 1 the German armies entered Poland. World War II had begun.

In the months that followed, the technique of the President was far different from what it had been from 1933 to 1938. It is altogether unlikely that Roosevelt wanted war, though some of his critics have so charged. Despite his bonhomie and his heartiness, he was essentially a private personality. He never wore his heart on his sleeve. He derived a kind of amusement from keeping people guessing. It is therefore very hazardous to write as if one knew his motives. It is clear, however, that in 1939 he thought that the issue was joined between the aggressor and the aggressed and that it was sound policy to help the aggressed. At the very outset of the struggle he made it clear that there was to be no moral neutrality. Contrary to Woodrow Wilson in 1914, he did not ask that the American people be neutral in thought. Indeed, he declared that such a thing was impossible—as it certainly was. And in addition he called Congress in special session to undertake a revision of the neutrality laws. He was careful to put his appeal for such a revision on a non-partisan basis. On September 20 he summoned the congressional leaders to the White House to discuss the situation. He told them that in his opinion the country would be more likely to keep out of war if the arms embargo were repealed. Secretary Hull attests the sincerity of this belief. To say this was by no means to quibble. It was merely to say that, if the democratic nations could win, there was less chance of the United States being involved than if Germany were victorious.

But the President was able to prevail only by making concessions to his critics. To meet the fear that a change in the neutrality laws might lead to involvement, Roosevelt accepted a new curb on his freedom of action. He was willing that the legislation to be enacted contain provisions for the establishment of war zones from which American vessels should be excluded. He was willing, too, that the prohibition on war credits and the cash-and-carry provisions of the law of 1937 (which had expired) should be reenacted. It was with these provisions that the repeal bill passed the two houses of Congress. The vote was hardly a non-partisan one. The final tally revealed only six Republicans in favor of the measure in the Senate and only nineteen in the House. The division clearly reflected the state of mind of the country at large. If the evidence of the polls is significant, there was probably a majority in favor of repeal; but there was no overwhelming sentiment for the ending of the arms embargo, and without the leadership of the President the thing might not have been done at all.

The American people had by no means been thoroughly aroused to the dangers of the European situation. It was possible to believe that the Allies would win the war anyway. The natural optimism of the American temperament suggested this conclusion. Not a few commentators on public affairs were ready to demonstrate just how it would happen. And many persons went further. The phrase,

The Deepening Crisis

"the phony war," which gained currency during the fall and winter of 1939/40 showed clearly enough how naïve many Americans were with regard to the course of events in Europe. The comparative calm that settled over the Continent after the easy conquest of Poland was interpreted not as a time of preparation but as an indication that the two sides were deadlocked.

Any such illusions were to be rudely shattered in the spring of 1940. In April came the invasion of Denmark and Norway. In May came the invasion of Belgium. In June came the march of German armies across France and the collapse of French resistance. In a few months the German armies had driven the meager British forces from the Continent and had brought all resistance to an end. Hitler was able, in the famous French Pullman car which had seen the German capitulation of 1918, to dictate terms as a conqueror and to dance with a terrifying delight at the completion of his conquest.

During all these months American diplomacy had been helpless to stay the course of events. The principal objective of the administration, so far as Europe was concerned, was to prevent the Italian dictator from coming to the side of his German comrade. Under-Secretary of State Sumner Welles was sent abroad to see what he could do to dissuade the government at Rome from entering the war. Thinly veiled warnings were sent to Mussolini that his intervention might be dangerous and that it would awaken much hostility in the United States. Efforts were also made to discover the explicit terms on which he might be bought off. But all these efforts were unavailing; and as the French armies collapsed in the north the Italians, in what was to be the most disastrous decision in recent Italian history, took up arms. Mussolini was playing the jackal at the feast prepared by the Germans.

It is almost impossible to exaggerate the sense of peril that permeated the minds of many Americans at the collapse of the democracies. By the end of May, 1940, the Committee To Defend America by Aiding the Allies had come into existence, and within six weeks more than six hundred branches of that organization had been formed. It was significant that the leader of this group was William Allen White, long-time Republican, the journalistic spokesman of the Middle West (where isolationist sentiment had been strong), the mellow and yet cautious friend of human liberty. It was also significant that the Committee To Defend America was, in the view of an influential number of westerners, by no means militant enough and that an organization called the Century Group was formed in New York to demand vigorous action regardless of the possibility of war. All things considered, there was force to the admonition of White to the President, "As an old friend, let me tell you that you may not be able to lead the American people unless you catch up with them."

The warning may or may not have been heeded. The President's own convictions may have been the determining factor in the great speech (the adjective is justified) which he delivered at Charlottesville, Virginia, on June 10. In ringing words he denounced the Italian "stab in the back." In explicit language he pledged to the democracies the assistance of the United States. "On this tenth day of June 1940, in this University founded by the first great American teacher of democracy, we send forth our hopes and our prayers to those beyond the seas who are maintaining with magnificent valor the battle of freedom. In our unity, our American unity, we will pursue two obvious and simultaneous courses; we will extend to the opponents of force the material resources of the nation and at the same time we will harness and speed up the use of those resources in order that we ourselves in the Americas may have equipment and training equal to the task of every emergency and every defense."

The Deepening Crisis

At the same time the President underlined the seriousness of the situation by two maneuvers, one in the domestic and one in the foreign field. He invited two eminent Republicans to join his cabinet as Secretary of War and Secretary of the Navy. One of these was Henry L. Stimson, who had been Secretary of State in the Hoover administration; the other was Frank Knox, who had been the Republican candidate for Vice-President in 1936. That these two men responded to the invitation is evidence of their own deep conviction of the peril of the time.

In the foreign field, the President's principal purpose was to prevent the tottering French government, or the government of Marshal Pétain which succeeded it, from giving up its navy to the Germans. There may never have been much chance that this would happen. At the moment, Hitler seemed to hope that he could make a satellite of France and was ready to be fairly reasonable. In any case, it may be doubted that the French naval service would have surrendered when it had never been defeated. But, it may be said to the President's credit, the handing-over of the French fleet might have seriously altered the balance of power on the sea.

In acting as he did, the President was reflecting a powerful movement in American public opinion. And this movement was well illustrated in the course of events in the Republican nominating convention of 1940. By the time it convened, Roosevelt had been renominated by the Democrats in defiance of the tradition against a third term. One might perhaps have thought that, since his own attitude was so vigorous, the opposition would nominate a candidate less committed to the cause of the Allies.

The most conspicuous possibility from this point of view was Senator Taft of Ohio. Though new to the Senate in 1938, Taft soon made himself the intellectual leader of the opposition. Active in debate, vigorous in speech, intellectually head and shoulders above most of his colleagues, often courageous, Taft's abilities were limited by his extreme partisanship and, perhaps (considering the times), by his essential conservatism. But neither of these limitations could have been expected to influence a convention of Republican politicians against him. There were other individuals, too, hopefully waiting for the lightning to strike, such as Senator Vandenberg of Michigan, who shared Taft's view as to Europe, and Thomas E. Dewey, who had won a reputation as prosecuting attorney in New York City and had come near to winning the New York governorship in 1938. But the convention took none of these men. A powerful ground swell of opinion, coming from outside the convention, resulted in the nomination of Wendell Willkie. Willkie had been a Wilsonian Democrat; he had not hesitated to speak out in favor of assistance to the democracies. On the other hand, as president of Commonwealth and Southern Power Company, he had fought the administration on the electric power issue. He was warm, friendly, fundamentally simple in his ideas, and without the taint of the professional. The choice proved that the Republican party had no mind to challenge the policy of Franklin Roosevelt in the foreign field.

Still more impressive evidence of American alarm was the action of Congress in the summer of 1940. For the first time in the history of the country a conscription law was enacted in time of peace. The movement for this law began as early as May and owed much to Grenville Clark, one of the founders with Theodore Roosevelt of the Plattsburg voluntary training camps in the war of 1914–17. At the outset both the War Department and the administration were distinctly cautious about accepting the idea, but after the fall of France a proposal for conscription was introduced in the House by James W. Wadsworth, a Republican from New York, and in the Senate by Edward R. Burke of Nebraska, an anti–New Deal Demo-

The Deepening Crisis

crat. Public sentiment developed rapidly behind the measure. On June 25 the figure of those who approved it in the public opinion polls was 59 per cent; on July 20 it was 69 per cent; and in late August it was 86 per cent. As the tide rose, the President began to assume a bolder position. On July 29 he asked authority to call out the National Guard for extensive training. A few days later he made a cautious statement in favor of selective service. He feared that if he took too positive a stand, the question might be made a party issue and that it might give the isolationists a handle for renewed agitation. He came out boldly only after Wendell Willkie had made it clear that he favored the measure and only a few days before the passage of the bill.

In one other great measure of the summer of 1940 Roosevelt acted under the prod of opinion rather than as the original proponent of a positive course. One of the primary needs of the hardpressed British in the summer of 1940 was for destroyers to protect their trade and to defend their coast against an anticipated German invasion. Almost half their destroyers had been damaged or demolished. As early as May a request for aid had been made to the United States. The agitation to meet this request was taken up by the Century Group, already mentioned, and the ingenious idea was brought forward that the transfer of the necessary naval vessels might be linked with the transfer of British bases on the American side of the Atlantic to the United States. The President was at first hesitant about this intriguing proposal. As in the case of conscription, he feared that his opponent for the Presidency might capitalize on any step he took. And he feared also to bring the question before Congress. But the tide of public opinion flowed rapidly; when Bullitt, American ambassador to France till the French collapse, made a speech in favor of the transaction, he received no less than 22,000 replies; the lawyers got busy with the interpretation of a previous statute which opened the door to the transfer by the President without new legislation; and word reached the White House that Willkie would probably not object to the idea. There was some difficulty on the other side of the Atlantic, for Prime Minister Churchill disliked the notion of a deal. But the Prime Minister's objections were overcome, and early in September agreement was announced. In exchange for the transfer of fifty over-age vessels (the British had asked for a hundred) the United States received, either on lease or as a gift, bases in the Western Hemisphere, extending from Trinidad on the south to Newfoundland on the north. Acting on his own authority, the President thus consummated a negotiation that underlined the purpose of the United States to render effective assistance to Britain and that ended any pretense of neutrality in the war raging in Europe.

The negotiation of the bases-destroyer deal was a master stroke. It was acceptable to the isolationists because the bases conceded by Great Britain would strengthen the defense of the hemisphere. It was equally acceptable to those who wished the United States to intervene more actively on the side of the democracies.

At the same time it was the signal for the crystallization of the opposition to the whole policy of aid to the Allies. A few days after the presidential announcement the organization of America First was announced. The movement had been incubating for some time, but it was taken up with a new sense of urgency in the fall of 1940. Although, as was natural, it found its largest body of support among Republicans (many such being distrustful of the President), it was by no means a partisan movement. It represented a point of view that was not destined to prevail but one that was held by such sincere public servants as Senator Taft and Chester Bowles, later to be a great ambassador to India. The America Firsters reasoned somewhat as follows: they maintained that the effect of war was to

The Deepening Crisis

undermine the democratic process itself and that the preservation of traditional liberties would be threatened by involvement in the struggle. They talked about the possibility of a negotiated peace. They argued that there was little physical danger to the United States from the activities of Hitler. In two of these three points they were certainly wrong. Time has shown that the democratic process in the United States was in no way undermined by war. A longer view also makes it clear that a negotiated peace was a complete impossibility in 1940. On the third point, they were right in the short perspective though wrong in the long one. We know now that Hitler was by no means eager for war with the United States and that he practiced what was for him great restraint in order to avoid one. But it is a totally different question whether, if the German dictator had once established his dominion in all of Europe with the weapons of modern war at his command, he would have been a comfortable—even a possible—neighbor for this country.

However this may be, the America First movement never really succeeded in halting the drift of American sentiment. It was never very broadly national; two-thirds of its membership came from within three hundred miles of Chicago. It never enlisted much support from labor or agriculture. Its national headquarters raised, during its entire existence, only $370,000. Despite the fact that its roster contained many well-known names, it never found a truly active chairman, and its executive director was a young man just out of college. There were vivid personalities connected with it, such as Colonel McCormick, the ebullient editor of the *Chicago Tribune*, Charles Lindbergh, the hero flyer of the Atlantic, and Hugh Johnson, the stormy petrel of the NRA. But McCormick was, after all, a thick-and-thin foe of the administration, Lindbergh's knowledge of foreign affairs hardly matched his knowledge of aeronautics, and Johnson was no popular figure by 1940. Furthermore, some of the groups that rallied to the support of the movement were more likely to provide the kiss of death than to invigorate it. Such were the Communists (until the summer of 1941), the Nazi sympathizers, and some anti-Semites. The leaders of America First tried earnestly to avoid association with such elements. But there was an unpleasant ring about some of Lindbergh's speeches, and in some places the intolerance displayed toward the America Firsters was such as to make public meetings impossible.

Partly as a result of the America First agitation, the election of 1940 was fought in an atmosphere in which apprehension of a German victory and of American involvement were curiously blended. Though there had been an immense change in the climate since the summer of 1939, there was still a strong desire to keep out of the war. Both candidates, as has been well shown by the late Charles A. Beard, catered to this feeling. Both equivocated and both made more sweeping assurances of their peaceful purpose than was consistent with the total situation. But whoever is disposed to be critical of this should remember the character of presidential campaigns in general. Very rarely are they fought on clear-cut issues. Very rarely are they distinguished for elevation of tone. The point to bear in mind is that the product is better than the process, that out of the distempers of the campaign period come a decision cheerfully accepted and an opportunity to go forward under leadership which in times of stress, as our history shows, has been adequate to its responsibilities.

The election was a victory for Roosevelt, who thus became the first third-term President of the United States. Confronted with a critical situation, a majority of the American people apparently believed that continuity of leadership was more important than doctrinaire attachment to a traditional principle. Although Roosevelt's victory was no such colossal triumph as that of 1936, it was nonetheless decisive and among the more emphatic indorsements of presidential candidates. And it opened the way for aid to the democracies, specifically, the passage of the lend-lease enactment of the winter of 1941.

By the time of the presidential election it was clear that Britain was hard pressed and that drastic measures were required in her behalf if the war was to be won. Public sentiment was rapidly crystallizing in favor of more forceful action. The President, released from electoral pressures, was ready to lead in a vigorous way. Toward the end of December he delivered his "arsenal of democracy" address, which foreshadowed sweeping measures of assistance to the British. A few days later he put before Congress what came to be known as lend-lease, a proposal for furnishing Britain with the materials of war, amounting to some $7 billion, and hinted at, but hardly provided for, repayment in the future. The President put forward his proposal as one that would keep war away from our shores and would promote the security of the United States.

There is in the phrase "lend-lease" a kind of disingenuousness that we should recognize. On the face of it, the supplies sent across the seas were unlikely to be restored or replaced. But it is quite another thing to accuse the President, as some of his postwar critics have done, of deliberately misrepresenting his program and of being at this time set on full involvement in the war. In 1941, as in previous years, he never cut himself off from public opinion. He was at all times aware—acutely aware—of the isolationists and America Firsters. In common with many other Americans, he may have sincerely believed that lend-lease would be enough, that the war could be won without the direct intervention of the United States. At any rate, there is no decisive evidence to the contrary.

In bringing forward his proposal, the President had correctly interpreted the temper of the nation. For two months the bill was debated in Congress. When the final vote was taken, the measure passed by 317 to 171 in the House and by 60 to 31 in the Senate. If, as seems reasonable to assume, Congress reflected the opinion of the country, there can be little doubt that the American people were ready to assist Britain. The conventional notions of neutrality had become outmoded; in the face of world aggression American sentiment was willing to align itself against the aggressor.

This is not to say that the American people in the early spring of 1941 were ready for war. Nothing is commoner in this world, for the individual or for the mass, than to nourish contradictory desires. When the lend-lease bill was passed, many Americans wanted both to avoid war and to assist the democracies, even at the risk of war. The America Firsters were still active. When Hitler, in the crowning folly of his mad career, in June, 1941, attacked Russia, the partisans of non-intervention were quick to argue that now the peril to the United States, if it ever existed, had been removed Why not let the two great totalitarian colossi destroy each other? What more desirable consummation than a weakened Germany and a weakened regime in the Kremlin?

That this line of reasoning appealed to many people was suggested by congressional action on legislation looking to the extension (for a period of eighteen months) of the service of soldiers already drafted. The bill to this effect passed the House by a majority of only one. Of the Republican members, 133 out of 154 declined to support the administration. They were joined by 65 Democrats, the largest number yet found in opposition. It is possible that a slightly shorter period of service would have rallied a stronger majority; but such a vote in the face of the demand of the War Department certainly indicated far from full acceptance of the thesis that the country was in immediate peril.

The Deepening Crisis

From the moment that lend-lease was enacted, the administration moved in the direction of implementing the new law by increasingly positive measures of assistance to the democracies. American naval and air forces were sent to patrol the Atlantic; the range of their operations was extended far to the eastward. On April 9 an agreement was signed with the Danish minister at Washington (who was naturally disavowed by the captive government at Copenhagen) by which the United States was permitted to occupy Greenland; three months later American troops replaced the British in Iceland. In a widely different area, advantage was taken of a favorable turn of military events to declare the Red Sea no longer a combat area, thus making it accessible to American shipping and relieving the British position in Egypt. The President, in the latter part of March and early April, was somewhat elliptical in his references to the problem of protecting the ocean lanes; but in a speech on May 27 he proclaimed an unlimited national emergency, spoke with candor of the measures that were being taken, and made it clear that goods must be delivered at all costs. On the other hand, the sinking of an American ship, the "Robin Moor," in the southern Atlantic was allowed to pass without any sharp demand upon the German government.

In August, 1941, came a highly dramatic event. President Roosevelt and Winston Churchill met together in Argentia Bay off the coast of Newfoundland and there drew up the remarkable document known as the Atlantic Charter. In every war, along with the severely practical problems that arise, an effort, probably a necessary and inevitable effort, is made to state its purpose in ideal and widely persuasive terms. There is always danger in such a course, for it is easy to arouse false expectations and grandiose dreams of the future. On the other hand, the instinct to give to a great national effort the character of a crusade for righteousness and peace is, perhaps, particularly strong in the Anglo-Saxon peoples. And it may be said that it is better to fix a high standard to live up to, even if one fails, than never to fix a standard at all. At any rate, this is what the Atlantic Charter, drafted by the two great leaders, sought to do. It was cautiously drafted; it was hardly a program in the literal sense of the word. But it spoke of the liberation of oppressed peoples, of freer trade, of economic collaboration, of a peace in which men might "live in safety and traverse the high seas and oceans without hindrance," of the eventual reduction of armaments. Since the United States was not yet in the war, it was an act of remarkable audacity on the part of the President thus to associate himself with the Prime Minister of Britain. Roosevelt undoubtedly sought to underline the identity of ideals and objectives between the United States and Britain.

Less than a month after the meeting at Argentia new dramatic developments took place. It was inevitable that the patrol of the Atlantic would sooner or later provide an incident, and in September that incident occurred. An American warship, which was carrying the mails to Iceland and which was also giving British ships information as to the position of a German U-boat, was turned upon by the latter, which fired a futile torpedo in its direction. The President promptly declared that hereafter American vessels, when they came in contact with German submarines, would not hesitate to strike the first blow and had been given orders to that effect. By his own act as commander-in-chief of the armed forces he thus began a kind of informal warfare against Germany. No decision made by him was more far-reaching than this; none stretched further his constitutional power. Yet, if the policy of lend-lease was sound, it seemed worse than futile to permit the supplies that were being sent to Britain to be sunk with impunity; and, if there seemed something disingenuous or at least metaphysical in describing all these activities as "defense," it was still true that they followed naturally enough from the initiation of the policy of active assistance to Great Britain. They gained a further sanction from the fact that in September the armies of Hitler were still advancing across the Russian plains and that the collapse of Russian resistance seemed a possibility.

A month later the President went further. He asked authority to arm the merchant vessels of the United States and suggested that the time might well have come to abolish the restriction by which American vessels, since 1939, had been forbidden to enter certain specified war zones. He insisted that it would be increasingly necessary to "deliver American goods under the American flag." "I say to you [Congress] solemnly," he declared, "that if Hitler's military plans are brought to successful fulfillment, we Americans shall be forced to fight in defense of our own homes and our own freedom in a war as costly and as devastating as that which now rages on the Russian front. Hitler has offered a challenge which we as Americans cannot and will not tolerate." It would be difficult to find a parallel for such bellicose language on the part of the Chief Executive of a nation not yet at war.

Congress was by no means united in support of the Chief Executive. A bill to arm the merchant ships of the United States passed the House on October 17 by a vote of 259 to 138, 113 Republicans opposing it. Before the Senate came to a decision on the measure, there were new incidents at sea: the United States destroyer "Kearny" was torpedoed on October 18; the "Reuben James" went to the bottom of the ocean on October 30. Acting under the influence of these new events, the Senate went further than the House; it attached to the House bill a provision permitting American ships to enter the waters from which they had been excluded under previous legislation. This measure giving the President all that he wanted passed the Senate by a vote of 50 to 27, but when it went back to the House, a bitter fight occurred. The final vote was hardly less than frightening as a symptom of national division; the House accepted the Senate bill by a margin of only eighteen votes.

To understand another international problem affecting the United States, we must go back and trace American-Japanese relations from 1939 to December, 1941. Many Americans had watched with aversion the advance of Japanese imperialism in Asia. The United States maintained a long-standing interest in China, an interest in part sentimental and religious, in part based on commercial considerations and perhaps on an exaggerated view of the significance of the China market, and in part concerned with the position of the Philippines. In view of all these facts, it need not appear wholly strange that American diplomacy was antagonistic to Japan. Yet the administration proceeded cautiously, certainly without intending to provoke an all-out quarrel with Tokyo. As early as 1938 it extended a loan to China; it strengthened its forces in the Pacific; it urged American manufacturers not to export planes to Japan. In August, 1939, it denounced the commercial treaty with Japan, and, after the necessary six months' interval, the treaty was formally pronounced no longer in effect. In July, 1940, the export of petroleum and scrap iron was restricted by the requirement of a special government license; a week later the export of aviation gasoline was banned.

In the meantime, the Japanese were moving steadily forward. In the early phase of the war Tokyo was cautious, but the fall of France emboldened the Japanese militarists to occupy northern Indo-China. More important, and indeed ominous, was the signing, on September 27, 1940, of a tripartite pact between Japan and Germany and Italy. In its phraseology this pact was defensive and bound the signatories to go to war only when one of them was attacked. But it recognized in all-too-clear terms the "leadership of

Japan" in the establishment of a "new order" in eastern Asia, and it was obviously intended to bring pressure to bear upon the United States. The pact was of course resented in Washington; the Roosevelt administration retorted by increasing its aid to the hard-pressed Chinese government of General Chiang Kai-shek.

Some among the President's intimates wished to see a more positive stand taken against Japan. There was talk in the winter of 1940–41 of sending planes to Chiang, with which he might bomb Japan. Mr. Dooman, the counselor of the American embassy at Tokyo, warned the Japanese vice-minister for foreign affairs that if Japan attacked Singapore, "the logic of the situation" might lead America into the war in the East, and his warning, though not instigated from Washington, was never disavowed. On the other hand, the President's military advisers were disposed toward caution, and some of them, notably Admiral Richardson, in command of the fleet at Hawaii, actually wished to see American naval forces brought back to the Pacific Coast. Others, like General Marshall, with their eyes on Europe, deprecated any strong action in the Orient. It was possible to issue warnings in vague general language, to add to the list of products under export control, and, more important, to begin staff conversations with the British looking to common action in the event of war. But more than this could not be done.

There were also divisions in the Japanese cabinet at this time. Prince Konoye, the premier, encouraged unofficial overtures at Washington aimed at relieving the tension. But the militarists, represented in the cabinet by Foreign Minister Matsuoka, were still in control, and it is unlikely that they would have consented to any terms that the American government could have accepted. The situation remained in an uneasy balance in the first months of 1941.

Two events were destined to unsettle the balance. In April

Matsuoka made a visit to Rome, Berlin, and Moscow. He was received with enthusiasm in official circles in the first two capitals, but, more significantly, he was able to bring about a neutrality pact with the Kremlin. By these means the Japanese rear was protected, at least on paper, against attack in case Japan wished to pursue her aggressive designs in the Pacific. In June came the German attack on Russia. The new turn of affairs for a short time disoriented Japanese policy, and some Japanese militarists wished to join Hitler in striking at the Soviet Union. Others, however, reasoned that the golden moment had arrived for action to the south, and the victory of this group in the cabinet was signalized by the occupation of southern Indo-China in the latter part of July, 1941.

There had been some conceivable excuse for the Japanese action in June, 1940, in moving into northern Indo-China and cutting off a possible route of supply to Chiang Kai-shek. But sending of troops south could only mean that new aggressive moves were contemplated. It made no sense except as a prelude to wider and wider acts of violence. And the Roosevelt administration responded with a far-reaching and portentous act of reprisal. On June 25 commercial and financial relations with Japan were suspended. The United States would no longer supply Japan with the means for the continuation of its career of conquest.

There is little doubt that this move, as later events demonstrated, confronted the government at Tokyo with an extremely critical situation. In particular, the ending of the trade in gasoline had a powerful impact. It meant that the Japanese war machine would have to look elsewhere for the supplies to carry on its purposes. It immensely increased the tension in American-Japanese relations and undeniably gave to the militarists a powerful argument in favor of aggressive action. Yet it rested upon a logical and easily understood hypothesis. The United States, by the summer of 1941, was straining every nerve to come to the aid of Britain. At such a time it was hardly defensible to divert to the Orient supplies that might be used by Japan for an assault upon the British position in the East. Furthermore, American public opinion had, for some time, increasingly insisted on stopping aid to Japan.

It is not quite right to say that the severance of economic relations ended all hope of accommodation with Japan. There were still important elements in Tokyo that dreaded a clash with the United States. It was not long after the imposition of the commercial embargo that Prince Konoye made his well-known proposal for a personal conference with President Roosevelt. Was it possible to come to an understanding at this late date? Could war in the East have been averted?

It cannot be stated dogmatically that the answer to these questions is "No." So close an observer and so accomplished a diplomat as Joseph Grew, American ambassador at Tokyo, believed then and continued to believe even after the end of the war that the overture made by Konoye should have been accepted. Many of those who have studied the question find themselves regretting the cold and rather rigid tone in which Secretary Hull dealt with the whole problem. However, one cannot be absolutely sure of Konoye's sincerity, still less that he could have dominated his own cabinet and forced the militarists to adopt a solution acceptable to the United States. Nothing in his previous career suggests that he was as strong as this would imply. But, in any case, on what terms could a settlement have been made? After supporting Chiang for three years, the United States could hardly abandon him, and Chiang himself had no interest in making an arrangement with Japan easy. The Japanese, on their part, could not be expected to withdraw support from the puppet regime which they had set up in China or to evacuate the country.

The New Age of Franklin Roosevelt, 1932–45

Whatever the judgment on Prince Konoye's proposal, it is certain that the American government was still by no means prepared to make positive commitments toward war. When the President and Churchill met at Argentia, one object of the British minister was to persuade the United States to warn Japan in definite and categorical language that an attack upon Britain in the Far East would be followed by military action by the American government. For a time it looked as if the President might follow such a course. But the statement agreed upon in the conference of the two political leaders was watered down before the President's return to Washington and further diluted before its communication to Admiral Nomura, the Japanese ambassador. The administration persisted in the policy that Roosevelt described as "babying the Japanese along." It certainly did not wish war in the Orient. The assertion to the contrary is among the legends of the period that ought to be emphatically denied.

On the other hand, the situation in the fall of 1941 was so poisoned by suspicion on both sides as to make understanding virtually impossible. Long before Pearl Harbor the State Department had broken the Japanese code, called "Magic." What it learned in this way was not calculated to increase its belief in Japanese good faith. As early as September 6, the Tokyo Imperial Conference approved proposals definitely involving preparations for war with the United States and Great Britain unless the United States ceased all assistance to China, agreed not to increase its forces in the Far East beyond existing strength, co-operated with Tokyo in providing Japan with necessary raw materials, and used its good offices in aiding Japan to establish closer ties with Siam and the Dutch East Indies. True, these demands were to be matched by concessions; but, whereas the concessions demanded of the United States involved definite acts in all but one instance, the Tokyo

126

government offered merely promises of good behavior in the future. Thus, the Japanese would *promise* not to use Indo-China as a base for operations against any neighboring country, would *promise* to withdraw troops from Indo-China when peace was established in China (possibly a Greek calends), would *promise* to guarantee the neutrality of the Philippines, would *promise* possibly to construe the tripartite treaty independently, and would *promise* not to take any action against Soviet Russia so long as that power remained neutral. The crude facts of the situation were that Washington was asked to back down from positions taken only after long consideration in exchange for mere paper assurances with regard to the future.

It is fair to say, therefore, that the situation had reached an impasse by the autumn of 1941. It was aggravated still more by the fall of Prince Konoye in October. Even then, strong elements in Japan wished to avoid a break, and General Tojo, who took Konoye's place as premier, seemed to show some willingness to continue the negotiations. But the new cabinet lost little time in accelerating the preparations for war, and the conversations between the Secretary of State and the Japanese ambassador, Admiral Nomura, accomplished nothing. Nonetheless, it must again be emphasized that the Roosevelt administration by no means desired to force things to a conclusion. On the contrary, a memorandum of the President (written about November 17) evinced a desire to resume commercial relations in some degree if the Japanese would send no more troops to the south and would agree not to be bound by the tripartite pact. Furthermore, a week or so later the State Department produced proposals that later became famous as the last effort to avert a clash. These proposals asked the Japanese to withdraw from southern Indo-China and to limit their forces in the northern part of that country. In exchange the United States would agree to lift restrictions freezing Japanese assets in America, and exports would be resumed subject to the control measures made necessary in the national defense. The proposal caused a howl of anguish from the Chinese, won little enthusiasm from the British, and met with a frigid reception from many circles in the United States. Secretary Hull soon dropped it in disgust. Though his action has since been the subject of harsh criticism, there seems little reason to believe that in any case it would have been acceptable to the Japanese. At the very time that it was under discussion, the Japanese squadrons were already sailing eastward to the attack on Pearl Harbor.

That attack came on the morning of December 7, 1941. More than 2,400 men were killed; more than 1,100 were wounded. Eight battleships were put out of action, and two were total losses. Three cruisers were more or less seriously damaged; three destroyers were wrecked; and most of the planes drawn up wing to wing on Wheeler Field were destroyed. The Japanese had executed one of the most successful surprise attacks in the annals of war.

Yet, from a broader point of view, the Japanese action was the maddest of follies, the kind of folly that only a non-democratic regime would be likely to commit. It is by no means certain that the American government would have brought the American people to all-out war if the United States had not been directly assailed. The Japanese would have been wiser to confine their attention to the British. There was little chance that the American navy from its Philippine bases on the Japanese flank could carry on effective action in the Far Pacific in the fall of 1941. By the shameless aggression on Hawaii, the militarists at Tokyo had succeeded in unifying American public opinion and bringing the most powerful nation in the world into the world struggle. The event was to prove that no grosser miscalculation has ever been made by military leaders than that made by General Tojo and his associates.

The Deepening Crisis

Nor is it quite certain how matters would have gone in Europe if Hitler and his Italian stooge had not responded promptly to the appeal of Japan to honor the Tripartite Pact. By declaring war on the United States the German and Italian dictators contributed in their turn to the crystallization of American public opinion.

We cannot take leave of Pearl Harbor without a word or two as to the responsibility for the disaster that overtook the American forces there. Absurd legends have been circulated with regard to the whole matter, of which the most ridiculous is that the President deliberately exposed the American fleet to attack with the object of bringing the United States into the war. General Marshall, the army chief of staff, one of the greatest figures of the war years, has been charged with grave laxity. The doubtful amenities of party politics have at times served to blur and distort the picture of what actually occurred.

The essential facts seem to be these. Ten days before the Japanese bombers winged their way over Pearl Harbor, the responsible authorities in Hawaii had been warned that the situation was critical and that hostilities might result. They were undeniably less than prepared for what actually occurred, although the possibility of an air attack upon this important base had been discussed as early as the winter of 1940/41. Yet in extenuation of their fault it might reasonably be said that no one expected the Japanese so soon. The not unnatural assumption, confirmed by much of the intelligence received, was that they would move southward toward the Kra Peninsula and Singapore. No one, either at Pearl Harbor or in Washington, believed that they could be as stupid as they actually turned out to be. It is possible to maintain that more explicit orders should have come from Washington between November 27 and December 7. And it is certainly one of the elements of tragedy in the situation that there was a delay in acting on the knowledge that came to the military and naval authorities in the morning of the fatal day. The news of the last Japanese note, which was the tip-off for war, was received about nine o'clock in Washington. Admiral Stark, the chief of naval operations, did not wish to send any special warning. General Marshall was out horseback riding that morning. He did not get the word until about 11:30 A.M. Had he been at his office an hour earlier, some at least of the losses sustained at Pearl Harbor might conceivably have been avoided.

There were also some strange miscarriages in Hawaii itself. The presence of a Japanese midget submarine was detected at 3:50 A.M.; it was not reported until six o'clock. The electronic equipment picked up the Japanese planes at seven o'clock, but the watch officer at the central station did nothing about it, expecting a flight of American B-17's. Errors of this kind occur in war, and tragic as the consequences of these particular errors may be, at the distance of fifteen years it is possible to find comfort in the fact that the very magnitude of the Pearl Harbor disaster unified the American people for the prosecution of the great struggle that was ahead.

The drama of the seventh of December has been often told. The day was a Sunday, and the Japanese representatives at Washington, Admiral Nomura and Saburo Kurusu, the latter a special envoy sent out from Japan, came to the State Department to present a last note from Tokyo. They were scheduled to be received at one o'clock, but through a delay in decoding they were not actually received by Secretary Hull until about 1:45. By that time the word of the Japanese attack had been received. In a speech filled with passion the Secretary denounced the note as "a document . . . crowded with infamous falsehoods and distortions—infamous falsehoods and distortions on a scale so huge that I never imagined any government on this planet was capable of uttering them." Stunned at the Secretary's indignation, the Japanese envoys could make no reply. Hull nodded toward the door, and Kurusu and Nomura departed without another word.

V I

The Home Front

That dramatic scene at the State Department ushered in four of the most remarkable years in the history of the United States, years not only significant in themselves but equally significant in their implications for the future. The American people had to meet the test implied in the mobilization and control of their political and economic resources at home and in combat on a world-wide stage. They could hardly hope to succeed abroad if they did not succeed at home first, and we may therefore begin our study of the war period by asking in what temper and by what methods they braced themselves for their problem and adventure.

A democratic nation sometimes suffers from internal division in time of war. This, indeed, had been the melancholy fate of France in 1939 and 1940. This had been the unhappy lot of the United States in the War of 1812. In the Wilsonian period, too, there had been dissent, though on no truly dangerous scale. The nation united in the fullest sense of the term, however, during World War II. The temporizing policies of the President, the shock of Pearl Harbor, the fact that there had been a substantial time for ethnic minorities to become assimilated since the sharp restriction on immigration in the early twenties—all these had something to do with the solidarity of the American people in the war. It was, no doubt, be-because of this solidarity that the problem of dissent was handled in so tolerant a spirit, and that there were almost no outbursts of the bitterness and intolerance that had flared forth from time to time in 1917 and 1918. But there is another consideration that helps to account for the absence of the proscriptive spirit. American radicals were behind the war effort. So long as Britain and Germany struggled, with the Russians on the sidelines, the Communists and their guileless followers had been the strident partisans of peace; but an abrupt change came over their attitude with Hitler's invasion of the Soviet Union, in June, 1941. The intellectual somersault they then performed was certainly lacking in moral dignity; it was disillusioning to all but the more naive of the fellow-travelers; but it had the effect of preventing an outburst of intolerance against the left. As to the right, only feeble elements among the German-speaking population of the United States were infected with nazism; there were almost no Fascist Italians; and it was possible to conduct the war with very little interference with personal liberty at home. The postmaster-general did indeed withhold mailing privileges in some cases, and the government dissolved the pro-Nazi organization known as the German-American Bund. But only a very few enemy aliens, that is, unnaturalized Germans and Italians, were interned. There was, however, one grave departure from the principle of tolerance. On the plea of military necessity the government removed 110,000 people of Japanese blood, many of them born in the United States and hence American citizens, from their homes on the Pacific Coast and forced them to remain in "relocation centers" during the war. The fact that in Hawaii a large Japanese-American population was left at liberty without damage to the national interest raises doubts as to whether this drastic procedure was necessary, violating, as it did, elementary civil rights.

The Home Front

On the level of party politics, the war was conducted with a minimum of tension. Partisan maneuvering, of course, occurred at times, but never did it present a real threat to the war effort. Never did it involve noxious interference with the management of the war on either the military or the diplomatic side. The President had contributed to this happy result at the outset by his appointment of Stimson and Knox in 1940. The chief assistants of these two men, James Forrestal, a Wall Street banker a with flair for public service, and Robert Patterson, a former judge of great intensity and energy, were admirable public servants whose administration of their departments left little room for criticism. As for Secretary Hull, he had long enjoyed great respect in Congress.

By 1944, it is true, the partisan spirit *did* revive. The Republicans had had some encouragement from the reaction against the administration which took place in 1942, when the Democratic majority in Congress was sharply reduced. They entered the campaign of 1944 with Thomas E. Dewey as their candidate and with some real hope of victory. But the campaign was not a virulent one; and Dewey conducted himself with restraint. There was nothing to rupture the national unity in what he proposed or advocated.

But, to go back to 1941, in order to maintain the national unity during the war it was both necessary and desirable to see that the nation's economic groups were kept happy. The success with which this was done is a testimony not only to the leadership of the President but also to the ability of congressional leaders to forge sound policies. Despite deficiencies in the war program, despite concessions to special interests, the general lines of action in the domestic field succeeded remarkably well in maintaining national morale.

Large sections of the business classes, as we have seen, disapproved the Roosevelt administration. At the beginning of the war in Europe there was considerable reluctance to venture capital in the war industries, and progress was slow until 1941. But an important step had been taken before Pearl Harbor; businessmen were permitted to depreciate their capital expenditures over a five-year period instead of over the usual twenty-year period. In addition, a substantial excess-profits tax was mitigated by a provision that after the war the expenses of reconversion could be used to offset the tax. Business entered the war, then, with positive encouragement from government to go ahead with the great enterprise of war production.

What American industry did under these conditions was phenomenal. Industrial production nearly doubled between 1940 and 1944. In the fields where great shortages existed, the results were truly astonishing. Take shipping, for example. Obviously the war required an enormous expansion of the American merchant marine. The ravages of the German submarine were met largely through the industrial genius of Henry Kaiser. In 1941 the number of merchant ships constructed was still small. It had increased over fivefold by 1944. The same astounding expansion took place in vessels of war. No less than 746 ships were produced between 1941 and 1944, in addition to 24,000 landing craft. Or take the record in aviation. The President's critics called him romantic when in 1940 he spoke of the manufacture of aircraft at the rate of 50,000 a year. But the figure was exceeded before the struggle came to an end. And the aviation industry, which produced 12,000 planes in 1940, produced 8 times that number in 1944!

What American industry did for the development of the nation's shipping and its airplane manufacturing is, of course, only part of the story. The needs of the army were met on a colossal scale (as, for example, by the manufacture of thousands of tanks and nearly 2,750,000 machine guns), and immense assistance was given to the country's allies. To the Soviet Union went trucks, tanks, and planes. To Britain went even greater quantities of the materials of war. It is safe to say that there had been no production even remotely approaching that of the United States in the annals of international conflict.

One of the great triumphs of American resourcefulness came in the field of rubber. The Japanese conquests in the Orient had cut off the principal source of supply of this all-important material. After an initial period of confusion a synthetic rubber industry came into being. By 1944 this industrial infant, assisted by the rationing of rubber for non-war uses and by the stockpile of natural rubber, was able to meet the needs of the armed services and keep the great military machine in full motion. A genuine national emergency had been effectively met.

The story of American war production might be almost indefinitely extended, but its indirect result ought to be considered here. It had been easy during the thirties to underrate the abilities of the American businessman. It was of prime importance now, when the nation faced a great problem, that he rose to the occasion. And the effects on his own morale were among the most significant results of the war itself. Business, which had been "in the doghouse" in the early years of the New Deal, now came back into its own.

But the maintenance of business morale was no more important than was the handling of the labor question. The year 1941 had been a turbulent one in this area of the nation's affairs. There had been a great coal strike only a little time before Pearl Harbor, and the settlement had represented a substantial concession to the demands of labor. It was obvious that the war itself might lead to new breaches of industrial peace. On the other hand, the outbreak of the conflict was met by the leaders of the workers in a patriotic spirit. The leaders of both the AF of L and the CIO joined in a no-strike pledge. Only two and a half weeks after the Japanese attack, a conference of business and labor leaders met in Washington and declared for the peaceful settlement of industrial disputes and the creation of a labor board to settle controversies which the disputants could not solve. In January, 1942, the President created the War Labor Board by executive order, with four members representing labor, four representing management, and four representing the public. The chairman was William H. Davis, a patent lawyer, whose ingenuity, humor, and patience fitted him eminently for his task.

The critical issue that confronted the board at the outset was the issue of union membership. Industry was by no means ready to accept the closed shop, the shop in which all workers must be members of the union. Labor forces, on the other hand, frequently pressed the demand. The board met the issue with a compromise that permitted settlement in case after case, a compromise called the maintenance-of-membership clause. Those who joined a union were required to remain members for the life of their organization's contract with management. On the other hand, the employers won a concession when it was agreed that there might be a fifteen-day period during which withdrawal from the union was permitted to the worker. As a result of understanding on this point, and no doubt also as a consequence of the war itself, the number of strikes substantially diminished in 1942.

A second problem that confronted the WLB was that of wages. Obviously, the immense spending by government would be likely to produce a period of inflation, and such inflation would bear heavily on the worker. As a partial remedy for this situation, the board hit upon a plan that came to be known as the Little Steel formula, since it was first applied in the steel industry. It stipulated that wage increases should keep pace with the rise in prices and that wage advances might be based on the increase in the cost of living between January, 1941, and May, 1942.

The Home Front

But any such settlement of the problem would have clearly been inadequate by itself. It depended upon the capacity of the government to prevent a further rise in prices, and the relative contentment of labor during the war period was therefore closely tied to the movement for price stabilization. At the very outset of the war an Emergency Price Control Act was passed and an Office of Price Control was set up under a vigorous and colorful administrator, Leon Henderson, who had once been a professor at Swarthmore College. In April, 1942, an order fixed maximum prices for consumer goods at the highest price charged during the preceding month. Yet it was clear that this would not be enough. Timing his move with great skill to take account of increasing breaches in the price structure, the President went further in September. Declaring that he might be forced to use his emergency powers if he did not receive the support of Congress, he demanded control over prices and wages on a sweeping scale. The act of 1942 limited wage increases to 15 per cent but left a wise and necessary loophole in cases where substandard or flagrantly inadequate wages prevailed.

Price control, however, could not stand alone. To prevent evasion of control and bootlegging of scarce goods, it was necessary to set up a system of rationing conducted by district, state, and local boards. To ease the pressure created by the enormous increase in the money supply resulting from government borrowing, it was necessary to restrict credit and to increase tax rates. Even so, by April, 1943, the President went further, issuing a still more drastic price control order, the "hold-the-line" order, virtually eliminating such discretionary increases as had previously been permitted. As a result of these various measures, a reasonably stable relationship between wages and prices was maintained until the end of the conflict. This was an impressive example of the power of a democratic government to deal with a central problem in time of war.

In general, the record of labor during World War II was a remarkable one. The principal difficulty came from the miners. John L. Lewis, the head of the United Mine Workers, had been and was in the war years one of the greatest figures in the history of the labor movement. His capacities were undoubted, and his views of the future of the industry were in many respects statesmanlike. In particular, he never opposed technological advance, the bogie of the less enlightened members of the labor movement. But by 1943 he had long been an embittered man, and he showed violent dislike for the President. He seemed to believe that, because the CIO, which he headed, had contributed to Roosevelt's victory in 1936, he owned the President body and soul. He had sided with Willkie in 1940 and had been one of the few big labor men somewhat isolationist in outlook.

Lewis sharply challenged the administration when the miners' contract with the operators ran out in the spring of 1943. Putting forward extreme demands, he refused to recognize the jurisdiction of the WLB, and in the last week of April the miners began to walk out, thus launching an industrial struggle that lasted through a great part of 1943. Twice in the course of the next five months the President seized the mines; the coal miners nevertheless refused to go back to work; and a final settlement was arrived at only after the miners received substantial concessions which, though nominally within the Little Steel formula, met the greater portion of Lewis' demands.

This exhibition of labor arrogance produced the natural popular reaction. As early as June and before the final settlement of the coal controversy, Congress passed the so-called Smith-Connolly Act, which authorized the President to take control of any plant or industry where a strike threatened the war effort and which imposed criminal penalties upon those who called or promoted a strike after governmental operation had gone into effect. At the same time, in industries not vital to the war, provision was made for a thirty-day cooling-off period and a vote of employees before a strike could go into effect. Finally, unions were prohibited from making contributions to campaign funds.

This legislation of 1943 stimulated political action on the part of the unions. The CIO formed a Political Action Committee that declared for a fourth term for the President and that made a strenuous effort in the election of 1944 to bring the labor vote to the polls. Though the Smith-Connolly Act prohibited direct contributions from unions, a great campaign of voluntary financing was organized, and a tremendous educational effort was set on foot. Moreover, the leaders of the PAC powerfully influenced the selection of a vice-presidential candidate on the Democratic ticket in 1944. When the President showed himself reluctant to accept Vice-President Wallace as a candidate, it was with their concurrence that Senator Harry Truman from Missouri was named. The choice was understandable, for Truman claimed a liberal record and had, besides, done yeoman work as the chairman of a committee to investigate the national defense. Though relatively inconspicuous, he had won the esteem and affection of many of his colleagues. The labor support given to the Democratic ticket was a major factor in Roosevelt's victory for a fourth term.

The increasing power of labor in the period of the war undeniably altered the balance of forces in the political and social order. But if one looks at the matter more narrowly, one sees the outstanding fact that during the war years there was an extraordinary industrial peace. The percentage of strikes declined, on the average, to one-third of that for the years just preceding. Over 400,000 voluntary agreements were approved by the WLB; more than 20,000 controversies were settled; and in only about a quarter of 1 per cent of the disputes was it necessary for the President to resort to seizure. Judged empirically, the program adopted must be accounted a great success in maintaining production and industrial harmony.

The achievement of American industry and labor in maintaining high levels of productivity during the war was matched by expansion in agriculture. Here, as in the other two cases, bait was held out to the group involved. Agricultural prices were permitted to rise to 110 per cent of parity. The results were phenomenal. By 1944 American farmers had brought under cultivation 30,000,000 more acres than in 1940; there was a tremendous increase in the quantity of wheat, cattle, and hogs; and the United States was able not only to provide for its domestic needs but to send immense quantities of foodstuffs to the Allies. A price would have to be paid for this great achievement: it was not to be easy to reverse the engines and resume more normal production when the war came to an end. Again, however, judged from the immediate point of view, a great success was achieved in meeting the demands of war.

A final group deserves special mention in connection with the development of American power in the years between 1941 and 1945. More than any previous war in history, World War II was a war of technology; and the role of American scientists, often supplemented by the role of European collaborators, was of fundamental importance in producing victory. The President himself was intensely alive to this problem. As early as June of 1940 he set up a National Defense Research Committee under the energetic and far-seeing leadership of Vannevar Bush. In 1941 the scope of this committee's activities was deepened and widened, and the wartime work of scientists was vital.

In the early period of the war the most significant scientific development was undoubtedly the widening use of radar. Radar, developed in Great Britain as an electronic means of detecting enemy planes, may well have saved the British from defeat in the great air battles of the summer and early fall of 1940. In the desperate submarine warfare of 1942–43, means were found through the so-called microwave to discover submarines on the surface far beyond the range of sight. The invention of the proximity fuse, another radar device, made it possible to burst shells nearer their target. When in 1944 the Germans launched the so-called buzz bombs on London, both ground radar and the proximity fuse played a large part in the defense.

There were countless other experiments with new weapons in the four years of war. Rockets attained a considerable importance and played a substantial role in the Allied invasion of France. A beginning was made in the field of guided missiles. But the truly sensational development was, of course, the invention of the atomic bomb.

Like all great scientific achievements, the atomic bomb owes much to the abstract thinker and is the product of the researches and speculations of scientists in many different countries. Yet it is ironical that the central idea that made the bomb possible was conceived by a gentle German Jew, Albert Einstein, who came as a refugee to the United States and whose name became famous throughout the world. This central idea was that matter was not inert and that changes taking place in matter might be made to result in the release of enormous amounts of energy. Einstein came to this conclusion and formulated an equation to explain it as early as 1905. In 1938 another development provided the next long step toward the new agent of destruction. Two German scientists subjected uranium, a radioactive substance, to bombardment by neutrons and found that the end product was the non-radioactive barium. The news of this discovery came to the United States through a Danish scientist, Niels Bohr, and was the subject of animated discussion at a conference of physicists gathered in Washington on January 26, 1939. At this conference it was suggested (and again by a refugee, the brilliant Italian Enrico Fermi) that in the process of thus transmuting uranium additional neutrons might be released so that a chain reaction could be set up which if repeated a sufficient number of times would release vast amounts of energy. Here then was the theoretical basis for the construction of the A-bomb.

The portentous possibilities of the new discovery were made known to the administration. Though several persons were responsible for this, it was Einstein who acted as the agent. It was he, among others, who grasped the immense issues involved and realized that, if the Germans took full advantage of the opportunities opened up by uranium fission, they might possess means of destruction such as the world had never seen. We may attribute then to this great thinker a leading role in prodding the government into action.

The first steps were slow. The President set up an Advisory Committee on Uranium under the Bureau of Standards in the summer of 1939. In June, 1940, as a result of an interview between Vannevar Bush and Roosevelt, the work was placed under the National Defense Research Committee, the body charged with fundamental research in connection with the war. Government funds were provided on an increasing though still modest scale. As the project widened, the army was brought in, in a limited way in the summer of 1942 and in the fullest sense in May, 1943.

It was a long way from theory to practice. A fundamental problem lay in the scarcity of uranium itself and in the fact that only a small part of the metal, known as U-238, could be used in the bomb. The story of the research that went on between 1939 and 1943 cannot be told in detail. It involved the labors of many, many scholars, English, Canadian, and French, as well as American. The direction of these researches in the United States was in the hands of Vannevar Bush, by virtue of his post as the head of the National Defense Research Committee, and of James B. Conant, the president of Harvard University, as the chief executive of the specific problems involved. Five different methods were employed to derive from uranium the necessary materials for the bomb. Three of these methods involved the separation from the metal (U-238) the small amount of fissionable material (U-235). Two involved the production of a new element, plutonium, from uranium. The work had to be conducted on a gigantic scale, and, before success was achieved, the expenditures amounted to $2 billion. At the atomic plant in Oak Ridge, Tennessee, a city of 77,000 people sprang up. Another big plant was erected on the Columbia River at Hanford, Washington, where grew a city of 60,000. And in New Mexico, about forty miles from Santa Fe, was developed a separate laboratory for those working on the design of the bomb itself, under the direction of J. Robert Oppenheimer. The technical problems involved in the manufacture of the bomb were gradually overcome, and on the night of July 16, 1945, the first atomic bomb in the history of the world was successfully exploded at Alamogordo, New Mexico. Thus a new age was ushered in.

VII

Arms and Diplomacy

When the war, by far the greatest contest in which the United States had ever engaged, began, the country's vast industrial machine had been set in motion, but it was very far from satisfying the immense needs of full belligerency. The draft had been enacted, but American armies were still being created rather than deployed. In the Orient the Japanese, for the first few months of the war, won victory after victory in the central and Far Pacific, overrunning the Philippines, Indo-China, the Malayan peninsula, Burma, Indonesia. and the island outposts, such as Wake and Guam, and even threatening Australia. Meanwhile, the great German war machine had advanced to the Don, and, though the Nazi forces were beaten back before Moscow, a powerful thrust launched in the spring of 1942 brought German arms, for the time being, to the Volga and was checked only by the heroic defense of Stalingrad. The situation in North Africa, too, was precarious. There the British, who had done well against the Italians in 1940 and 1941, found themselves confronted with one of the ablest of German generals, Marshal Rommel. In the late spring of 1942 British forces were driven back from Tripolitania almost to the frontier of Egypt, and Mussolini looked

144

forward, with the assistance of his German friends, to a triumphal entry into Alexandria. Finally, no adequate preparations had been made against the German submarine, and the U-boats ranged up and down the Atlantic Coast and waters of the Caribbean. Vessels were sunk within thirty miles of New York, off the coast of Florida, and even in the vicinity of the Panama Canal. More ships were sunk than built in the initial period of the war.

So it had been in World War I as well. Nineteen hundred seventeen had been as gloomy as, perhaps even more gloomy than, 1942. The French offensive under General Nivelle in April of that year had been beaten back, and there had been mutinies in the French army; the summer saw the gradual dissolution of Russian power; the fall witnessed the crushing defeat of the Italian armies on the Piave; and November saw the entry of the Bolsheviks into power; and the beginning of Russian overtures for a separate peace with Germany. Yet the broader picture, and the longer view, were to tell a different story; and it is a fact to remember that, so far at least in modern history, the staying power of the great democracies has brought them eventual victory. The time margin may not be so generous in the future; but the awareness of peril is in these days more acute; and it can at least be said that this nation is not likely to face a new war as little prepared as it was in 1917 or even in 1941.

The danger from the Japanese was in a sense the more immediate, and, despite many instances of American gallantry—the heroic defense of the Filipino fortress at Bataan and of Wake—there was little to cheer about until May and June of 1942. In these months were fought the remarkable battles of the Coral Sea and of Midway, both new in the history of sea warfare. The entire action in the Coral Sea was fought from aircraft carriers, and neither fleet ever caught sight of the other. At Midway, though the land-based bombers on the American-held island played a gallant part, the carriers again had the central role. Coral Sea inflicted heavy losses upon the Japanese—losses, however, which were nearly balanced by the American ones; but Midway was, in a sense, the turning point of the Pacific War. It broke the force of a Japanese invasion fleet headed toward Hawaii; and it ended Japanese offensives in the Pacific.

In the meantime, the central question had to be answered in Washington. What should be the grand strategy of the war? Should the major effort be directed against Germany or against Japan? Not, of course, that anyone advocated inertia in one field and total commitment in another; the question was relative but nonetheless of transcendent importance. It was decided in essence that Germany was the more dangerous enemy. This was the view of the President's most trusted military advisers; but on at least one occasion when they were inclined to weaken, they were stiffened by the President himself. In retrospect the argument seems to this writer conclusive: in Europe the United States had effective allies; in Asia only Chiang Kai-shek, a very ineffective one, and the broken power of Britain. Moreover, in Europe the United States faced a power whose mighty technological resources and ingenuity might be used, with the progress of invention, to terrorize the world.

It need hardly be said that Prime Minister Churchill approved of this decision; indeed, he lost no time after Pearl Harbor in crossing the Atlantic to urge such a course of action on Roosevelt. And thus began the close association of these two remarkable men and an intimacy that, despite profound divergences of view (for Churchill was fundamentally a Tory and an imperialist and Roosevelt a liberal and an anticolonialist), lasted with only occasional spats until the death of the President.

Arms and Diplomacy

But, granting that the war in Europe must be pressed, how was this to be done? Here the American chiefs, from the beginning, had a clear idea of what they wanted: a cross-Channel invasion of the Continent in force, which would engage large numbers of Germans while the Russians kept them equally busy in the east. For Churchill this prospect was less inviting; he remembered the days of dreary World War I trench warfare and the staggering losses in that warfare. Although he never dared—or perhaps desired—to oppose the American plan, he was extremely cautious about the timing and disposed, as we shall see, to alarums and excursions in other areas. It was partly because of him, partly because it was patently impossible to launch a successful invasion of France in 1942, and obviously necessary to get something started, that the invasion of North Africa was determined upon for the fall of that year.

The United States, after the fall of the French parliamentary regime and the installation of Marshall Pétain as chief of state, had the wisdom (despite the shrieks of some of the doctrinaires of the left) to maintain relations with the new regime. As a result, it was possible by an agreement with General Weygand, Pétain's subordinate, to keep contact with the French in Morocco and Algeria and, in distributing economic assistance, to learn a great deal about the situation there. It was possible, also, to get in touch with French officers who were willing to co-operate in the invasion. The enterprise was set for November, 1942.

The commanding general of this first offensive against the Germans had been only a lieutenant colonel at the beginning of the war. But General Marshall, the chief of staff, had put him in charge of the operations section of the staff, and there he had won the General's confidence. He had then been selected, over many higher-ranking officers, to take charge of the forces being mobilized in Great Britain; and there he had shown those remarkable personal qualities that were to make him a great figure in the future. The name of this officer was Dwight D. Eisenhower.

What were Eisenhower's gifts? Modesty was one of the most attractive of them, modesty and a superlative capacity to work with others. A genuine conviction of the necessity of international co-operation to win the war was another. Wisdom in the selection of subordinates was a third. Resolution was a fourth. And an eye for the essentials was a fifth. No general, however distinguished, does his work alone. No general is exempt from mistakes. But in selecting Eisenhower for this job, Marshall and the President did well. They could hardly have suspected that they were paving the way for this man to become President.

The North African campaign was begun in November, 1942. It was a brilliant achievement, involving, as it did, a vast amphibious operation carried on at a great distance from army bases and across an intervening ocean. In its initial stages it was successful; Algeria and Morocco were occupied with relatively little fighting; but then the Germans riposted vigorously. They were able to prevent a swift thrust toward Tunis; and it was not until May, 1943, that their forces, caught between Eisenhower and the British General Alexander, whose troops were advancing westward from Egypt, were compelled to withdraw completely, with losses amounting to 350,000 men. The conquest of Sicily followed; and the month of July was marked by the collapse of Mussolini's regime. When comparing the efficiency and wisdom of totalitarian and democratic regimes, it is well to reflect upon the fate of this unhappy dictator who brought his country into a war that the great majority of Italians undoubtedly wished to avoid.

The conquest of Sicily was followed by the invasion of southern Italy. The Allied advance was checked some distance south of

Arms and Diplomacy

Rome in January, 1944; but, in any case, in the American view, the thing to do was to prepare the great cross-Channel invasion for 1944. Though Churchill was still by no means convinced, he could hardly resist, and the most formidable enterprise in military history went forward. It is difficult to exaggerate the technical problems involved in landing a great army on a widely defended coast against a formidable enemy. Vast stores of supplies were brought together; two fabricated harbors were constructed; landing craft of entirely new types were brought into play; a tremendous air force was organized. On the day set for the invasion, the weather was stormy; to delay more than a day might have meant postponement for at least a fortnight. With better reports coming in, Eisenhower made the fateful decision to chance it on the next day, June 6, and on that day the Americans landed on the coast of France. The courage and decision shown by the commanding general were to be amply rewarded. The battle of Normandy lasted from June 6 to July 24. The Allied airplanes, far exceeding the German planes in numbers, played a vital part by disrupting communications; the Germans had been taken by surprise; the great American and British effort had been synchronized with a terrific offensive on the Russian front.

By the end of August Paris had been liberated, amid great rejoicing; an American army had been landed in the south of France and was marching victoriously northward, forcing the withdrawal of large German forces in the western part of the country. By autumn all France had been cleared of the Nazi hordes, while on the left flank of the American armies the British forces under General Montgomery cleared Belgium and a part of Holland. Checks came, however, at the end of the year; the Germans made one last and really threatening effort in December in the tangled region of the Ardennes. Eisenhower reacted promptly; he put part of the American force under the command of General

Montgomery to strengthen the defense on the north; and by the middle of January the danger had been averted. In March came the decisive advance across the Rhine. At that great line of defense the Americans discovered a bridge still standing at the little town of Remagen, and troops poured across before the Germans could organize their resistance. Once this was accomplished, other bridgeheads were established, and the armies of the Allies advanced victoriously toward the Ruhr and through the mountains of Würtemberg and Baden. It was clear that the end was near. It came with the dramatic suicide of Hitler in his bunker in Berlin and with the signing of the articles of capitulation near Rheims by a caretaker regime May 7.

We should not leave the campaign in Europe without raising some general questions as to the grand strategy of the war in that theater. One question that has been and will be asked is whether it would have been possible, because of the immense and increasing Allied preponderance in the air, to have reduced Germany by bombing alone. The matter is in dispute, but it is worth noting that German production actually increased during 1943 and 1944, despite the violence and frequency of the British and American air raids. It was rather by the disruption of transportation and by the devastating blows dealt the German oil supply that the air force appears to have performed its greatest service. These activities played a vital part in making the invasion of the Continent a success.

Another question concerns the possibility that the Allies might more vigorously have exploited their Italian successes. Prime Minister Churchill had always been fascinated by the idea of an attack from the south; he had played with the notion of sending the Allied forces in Italy northward into the Lombard plain, and thence possibly moving northward through the Semmering Pass toward

Arms and Diplomacy

Vienna. He believed that more advantage should be taken of what he called "the soft under-belly" of the enemy. There was never any real possibility of this expedient's being tried; nevertheless, it is worthwhile to analyze the matter. In reality, the "soft under-belly" was not soft at all; the route through the Alpine passes and the so-called Ljubljana gap toward the Austrian capital would have involved the most difficult kind of fighting. In addition, it was the firm opinion of the American high command that some of the troops fighting in Italy should be detached for a landing in southern France, which would give the armies of General Eisenhower and General Montgomery more supply bases and which would make possible a linking-up of these troops with the forces in the north. On the broadest ground, the American point of view seems sound. It is true that the ideas of Churchill would have given the democratic nations a stronger position in Austria and in the Balkans; but it is difficult to see how any such enterprise could have failed to slow up the advance of the great armies driving toward the industrial heart of Germany. Had it been tried, the Russians, who were all this time advancing against a steadily weakening opposition might well have found themselves at the end of the war in possession of a far larger part of Germany than was actually the case.

Still another controversy over grand strategy had to do with General Eisenhower's decision to advance on a broad front into Germany. Might it not have been better to hold back the American armies and to let General Montgomery drive ahead swiftly from the Low Countries and the lower Rhine toward the German capital? Here again the answer must be in some part speculative. But to check the onward drive of the American troops, of the dashing Third Army under General Patton and the First Army under General Hodges, and to limit these armies to a much less ambitious operation would have been psychologically difficult, to say the least. And there is no certainty that any such operation would have succeeded.

However this may be, the campaign of 1944–45 was certainly one of the most remarkable in military annals. To march in less than a twelve-month period from the peninsula of the Cotentin in western France to the border of Czechoslovakia, to destroy a large part of the German army in the process—this was indeed an achievement. It is true and important that the forces of Hitler were at the same time deeply engaged in withstanding the Russians in the East. But, making all allowance for this fact, the success was still of the first order. It was the product of an immense technological effort, of the growing air superiority of the democratic nations, of the courage and ability of the British and American commanders, and of the fighting spirit of the forces on the ground. It was a striking demonstration of the ability of a democratic nation to muster its resources and to win through to final victory.

We must turn from the war in the West to the war in the East. There the greater part of the burden fell upon the United States alone. Australian and New Zealand forces engaged in the campaign in New Guinea (of which we shall shortly speak); there were British forces in Burma and Chinese forces in China; but the preponderant effort was made by the United States.

We have already seen how in the first months of the war the Japanese carved out for themselves a great empire in the Pacific. But after the Battle of Midway they were never able to take the strategic offensive again. In the four years that followed, they were gradually pressed back until they, like the Germans, ended in utter collapse. What are the leading events in this remarkable story?

The broad strategic story of the war in the Orient is easily stated. There were two commands: the Pacific command, under the direction of Admiral Nimitz and Admiral King, the naval forces of

Arms and Diplomacy

which were reinforced by marines and later by a number of army divisions; and the Southwestern command, under the leadership of General Douglas MacArthur. In the early stages of the war these two commands operated to a large degree independently; it was not until the autumn of 1943 that their large-scale movements were carried on in conjunction. Until that time General MacArthur was chiefly engaged in clearing the important island of New Guinea, with its threat to Australia. The navy and its supporting forces nibbled away at the Japanese Pacific barrier and advanced closer to the heart of the new empire.

Let us look first at the New Guinea campaign and at its commander. Douglas MacArthur was a soldier's soldier. His father had been a distinguished military man, and young MacArthur had never contemplated any other than a military career. He had been at the head of his class at West Point; he had been a division commander in World War I and afterward had been sent to the Far East. Save for a few years as chief of staff, he spent most of his career in this area. He had been commander of the Filipino and American forces in the Philippines at the outset of the war, had conducted the heroic retreat and defense of Bataan, and had, on orders of the President, left the island by submarine to take up his new command in Australia. Thence he was to direct the operations which we must analyze.

These operations were conducted with great skill. The General could proudly say that few commanders had done more to spare their troops and at the same time inflict greater losses on the enemy. With meager forces, with an unprecedented problem of supply (which had to be solved in large part by supply from the air), with the grueling conditions of jungle warfare and the concomitant danger of disease, he was able in the campaign initiated in the fall of 1942 to push back the Japanese, isolate them from their comrades, and in the course of a year and a half retake the whole island of New Guinea. Like Eisenhower, he knew how to choose excellent lieutenants, and the names of General Kinney and General Eichelberger, in command, respectively, of the air forces and ground forces under MacArthur's control, deserve to be given more notice than they usually received in the commanding general's dispatches. MacArthur was particularly well fitted for the task assigned to him. His subsequent career suggests that he would have been far less successful in the quasi-diplomatic job required of the commanding general in Europe.

Until 1944 the major role in the operations in the East fell upon the navy and its supporting forces. The first great theater of operation was the island of Guadalcanal in the Solomons on the periphery of the Japanese empire. American forces were thrown into Guadalcanal in August, 1942. Few struggles have been more savage than that which followed. The Japanese made every effort to displace the invaders. The Americans had not been long ashore before the Japanese won a striking victory, in the Battle of Savo Island, over the supporting naval forces. A series of hard-fought naval engagements followed. At one time the marines on the island even lost control of the airfield that formed an essential element in their defense. The supply problem was terrific. Yet by the end of November the island was secure. In the last of the Guadalcanal naval engagements (with Admiral Halsey in command of the American forces), the Japanese were decisively defeated; they lost much of their reserves; their morale suffered; and after November, 1942, they were, until the critical battle of 1944, unwilling to risk their fleet against the Americans. The initiative in the sea war had passed to the United States.

The Americans made good use of that initiative. Their air power increased, and the American aviators far outmatched the Japanese. With relative impunity American submarines destroyed an enormous number of Japanese commercial vessels. And the navy and the marines embarked upon an island-hopping campaign that gradually contracted the Japanese periphery by the occupation of strong points while leaving other such points subject to constant air attack, withering on the vine.

By the summer of 1944, however, with the conquest of New Guinea, new and fundamental questions of strategy arose. The navy advocated action against Formosa or the Ryukyus, with an attack by MacArthur in Mindanao. General MacArthur, on the other hand, no doubt in part influenced by considerations of prestige and of sentiment, wished the next great thrust to be directed toward the reconquest of the Philippines. The controversy that ensued was settled by the President himself in one of his rare personal decisions, but with the concurrence of the joint chiefs of staff. After all, the only considerable body of land forces in the Pacific area was under MacArthur's command, and it seemed reasonable to give that general's views special weight. In joint operations the way was cleared for the attack on the Philippines by the occupation of the key posts of Morotai and the Peleus. On October 14, 1944, the American forces landed on the Filipino island of Leyte. The effect of this landing was to bring the Japanese navy into action in what was one of the greatest and most decisive battles of the war, the battle of Leyte Gulf. The Japanese put forward a terrific effort, sending three task forces into action, and fought desperately with their suicide planes, the Kamikaze, in an effort to destroy the American naval forces. They did inflict heavy losses, but the price paid was fatal. Their entire carrier service was wiped out; they lost three battleships, eight heavy cruisers, five light cruisers, and nine destroyers, or more than half of their entire navy. They were never again able to fight an action at sea, and their defeat in the war was now foredoomed.

We may, therefore, pass lightly over the brilliantly conducted operations by which General MacArthur conquered the Philippines and the costly battles further north which drew the net closer around Japan. Devastating air raids on the mainland of Japan now became a matter of course; the rest of the Japanese navy was sunk; their merchant marine was almost annihilated; and the situation of the Japanese became desperate. But they hung on tenaciously as, in the winter of 1945, the American forces moved still nearer the core of the Empire with the seizure of Iwo Jima and Okinawa, the last only four hundred miles from Tokyo. The Americans were preparing for an actual invasion of the mainland of Japan when the end of the war came.

Franklin Roosevelt was not destined to see the great events that terminated the struggle in the Orient. He suffered a massive cerebral hemorrhage and never recovered consciousness, dying on April 12. It was left to a new and unprepared President, Harry Truman, to make the last crucial decision in the Far East, to take the awful responsibility for the dropping of the atomic bomb and, on the other hand, to ease the final capitulation of the Japanese by permitting them to keep their Emperor.

The military and naval events of 1941–45 constitute only a part of the war story. As we have narrated them, they tend to place too much emphasis on the role of America in the struggle. After all, the war was a world war, not an American war; and it is necessary to see it in a world perspective. It could not have been won without the assistance of America's allies.

It is not necessary to say much about the position of the states of Latin America. Thanks to the wise policies of the thirties, most of them associated themselves with the United States in the conflict. Those in the Caribbean area, almost without exception, declared war and were before long followed by Mexico and by Brazil; most of the rest severed relations with the Axis, and only Argentina, congenitally jealous of the role of the United States, remained throughout most of the struggle not only aloof but the center of Nazi intrigue. In the physical sense, the addition of the New World states to the ranks of the Allies was not of the first importance, though the entry of Brazil facilitated the development of an important line of communication across the Atlantic. But as sources of raw materials the Latin-American republics were of prime significance; the friendship of the little countries near the Panama Canal was obviously highly desirable; and the moral effect of these new adhesions to the democratic cause was not to be overestimated.

Obviously, of far greater importance was the role of Britain. The gallant resistance of the British in 1940 and 1941 made victory possible. The British position in North Africa proved to be of great importance. The British part in the invasion of the Continent was central. On the whole, it is remarkable with what extraordinary smoothness the joint operations of the two English-speaking nations were carried on. There were differences of opinion as to strategy, as we have seen; there were occasional moments of tension in the numerous conferences of Roosevelt and Churchill; but in the fundamental sense there was a degree of co-operation never before paralleled in the relations of two independent peoples.

The political differences that did exist were for the most part glossed over. Franklin Roosevelt reflected majority sentiment in his dislike of that vague thing called British imperialism; and at times he needled the Prime Minister, provoking him to real indignation. But, for the most part, the controversy was kept in the background; and only once did Churchill's indignation break forth in public, when he declared in Parliament that he had not become the King's Prime Minister in order to "preside over the liquidation of the British empire." The anti-imperialism of the President, so his critics of today frequently assert, set in motion forces highly inconvenient for the West; but it is extreme to attribute the rising self-consciousness of the so-called dependent peoples in the world today to the influence of a single man. It seems likely, indeed—if not certain—that, Roosevelt or no Roosevelt, the contemporary world would have to reckon with a militant nationalism among the restless populations of Africa and Asia.

It is sometimes said that the President and the Prime Minister made one of the capital mistakes of the war in the conference which they held at Casablanca in the winter of 1942. There they promulgated the so-called "unconditional surrender" doctrine, and the argument runs that it contributed to the prolongation of the conflict by stiffening the resistance of the enemy. It is difficult to see how this argument holds. Certainly, the Italians capitulated quickly enough when they were under pressure; indeed, in 1944 and 1945 Italian contingents were fighting with the democracies. As for Germany, the fact is worth noting that "the unconditional surrender" idea did not prevent the formation of a plot against Hitler, which nearly succeeded in assassinating the dictator in the summer of 1944. Only chance saved the Fuehrer from being fatally injured by a bomb introduced into his own headquarters and exploded at a conference at which he was present. But apart from this, was it not sound doctrine to refuse to negotiate with this sinister tyrant and to insist upon total capitulation so long as he remained in power?

Errors, however, are inevitable in large affairs, and in two matters in which they acted in concert, the President and the Prime Minister undoubtedly erred. One error, the commitment to the drastic reduction of Germany's industrial power (the so-called Morgenthau plan), made at Quebec in the fall of 1944, was soon redressed; in retrospect it seems hardly believable that it should have been committed. The other was more serious. Long before the end of the war, agreement had been reached with the Russians as to the zones of occupation for the great powers at the end of the war. The effect of this agreement, in practice, was to deliver over to the tender mercies of the Kremlin areas which had been overrun by the American forces and which might have been preserved for freedom.

We see this kind of thing, however, in a perspective today different from that of the war years. After all, the role of the Russians in the war was fundamental. They were engaging enormous German armies, and their collaboration was essential. There was always the specter of still another bargain between the Nazis and the Communists, such as that actually engineered in 1939 before the invasion of Poland. Good relations with Stalin were a matter of prime importance. And good relations were extremely difficult to maintain. At the outset the Communists were (to put it mildly) anything but gracious in their attitude toward the West. On the contrary, they were highly suspicious, and there was much futile wrangling in 1942 and during part of 1943. In a sense, this is understandable. It was no doubt difficult for the men in the Kremlin to appreciate the enormous task of preparation necessary before American power could be brought to bear in Europe, and, being themselves ready to double-cross their allies if expediency suggested such a course, Stalin and his associates naturally attributed similar purposes to Great Britain and the United States.

But in the spring of 1943 the diplomatic skies seemed to clear a bit with the abolition, on paper, of the Communist international, and in August of that year Secretary Hull rode in an airplane for the first time in his life to confer with the Soviet potentates in Moscow. At this conference a declaration pledged the three great powers to fight the war to a decisive end; and the Russian dictator assured the Secretary that when the struggle was over in Europe, the Kremlin would turn its arms against Japan. In December came a far more dramatic manifestation of unity. Roosevelt, Churchill, and Stalin met together in the Iranian capital of Teheran. In four days of conference the plans were developed for the great invasion of the Continent by the forces of the West, and for the co-ordination of Russian military movements with this invasion; many other important questions were discussed, and the three statesmen parted on the best footing that they were ever to reach during the whole period of the war. Rifts occurred from time to time thereafter, but on the whole, 1944, the year of the Allied landing in France and of sweeping victories over the Germans, marked the peak of co-operation with the Kremlin.

More disputable is the course of events at the second meeting of the three great leaders, at Yalta in the winter of 1945. Here, too, there was a façade of unity, but ominous signs of division were already appearing, soon to be followed by events more disturbing still. It was at Yalta that President Roosevelt made the famous deal with regard to the entry of Russia into the war against Japan. Stalin demanded as the price of his co-operation a free port in Manchuria, railway rights in the same province, the possession of the Kurile island chain stretching eastward into the Pacific and of southern Sakhalin off the northern provinces of Japan, and the right of the Russians to occupy North Korea in the course of their intervention. These various concessions were made by the President acting in the utmost secrecy and without the participation of his Secretary of State. They represent an extraordinary exercise of the power vested in the Chief Executive.

The agreements made at Yalta have been the subject of the most violent controversy. It has been stated with much force that it was not necessary to make any concessions whatsoever; the Russians would, without them, have been glad to seize what loot they could from Japan when the war in Europe was over. It has been contended that Roosevelt at Yalta sacrificed the interests of a friendly power, China, to the insatiable ambition of the Russian dictator. It has been suggested that he acted unconstitutionally, or at any rate was guilty of a political impropriety; and in the heat of partisan argument it has been charged that Yalta paved the way for the loss of China to the Communists in the years after the war.

This last charge is wholly unfounded. The others have an undeniable force. But let us state the case from the President's point of view. In answer to the first of these criticisms just mentioned, it may be contended that Roosevelt gave away nothing that the Russians would not have been able to take anyway; in answer to the second, the sacrifice of Chinese interests, it should be noted that the Nationalist government of Chiang Kai-shek freely accepted an arrangement similar to that made at Yalta in exchange for Soviet support of its own regime; in answer to the third, it may be claimed that the President acted within the scope of his war powers. However we evaluate the one and the other side of the argument, one thing stands out clearly: the *motive* of the President was to shorten the war. In February, 1945, it was the opinion of his leading military advisers (incorrect in fact) that the conflict with Japan would entail, in all probability, the invasion of the main island and bloody sacrifices in the course of such operations; and it was these sacrifices that the President sought to avoid.

From another point of view Yalta certainly led to early disillusionment. An agreement was made there which provided for the setting-up of democratic governments in Eastern Europe; yet the ink was hardly dry on the document before Andrei Vishinsky appeared in Bucharest, the Rumanian capital, which had fallen to Soviet arms, and installed a regime under Communist domination. And what was done in Rumania was to be done in a slower tempo in Bulgaria, in Hungary, and in Poland. In nothing did the Soviet government show its faithlessness more than in these transactions.

The New Age of Franklin Roosevelt, 1932–45

The tension between Russia and the West was again illustrated in April when the war in Europe was drawing to an end. Stalin thought he saw, in the negotiation of an armistice with the Germans in Italy, an attempt to betray the Soviet regime. He intervened rudely in the discussion, and he was answered with considerable asperity by the President himself. Though in the last days of his life Roosevelt was still optimistic about being able to come to some kind of working agreement with the Kremlin, those who knew Russia better (as, for example, Averell Harriman, our ambassador at Moscow) were by no means cheerful about the future.

Problems no less grave and frustrations no less extreme were to be found in American relations with the China of General Chiang Kai-shek. Time was to reveal with dramatic starkness the weakness of his regime, which was never quite so strong as Americans wished to believe. Even as early as 1937 the Chinese Communists were in control of a substantial area in China. Chiang himself was driven by the Japanese invasion from the valley of the lower Yangtze and had to set up his capital in the mountain province of Chungking. There he fell more and more under the influence of reactionary landholders and of elements that by no stretch of the imagination can be described as democratic. His military forces were ill disciplined and ill supplied; his reluctance to engage them against the Japanese and his preference for holding them in reserve against the Communists were marked. The government of the United States did much to try to strengthen him. It urged successfully the association of China with the three great powers in the Declaration of Moscow in October, 1943. At Cairo, shortly before the Teheran conference, President Roosevelt conferred with Chiang, and it was agreed that Formosa should go back to China at the end of the war. Military assistance was also furnished; a strong and energetic commander was sent out to the Far East in the person of General Stilwell, and, despite immense obstacles, an effort was made to help the Chinese over the famous Burma Road. But Chiang quarreled with Stilwell; the Chinese general resisted the efforts to improve his forces; and in 1944, when the war was going well on almost every front, the Japanese won important victories in China and were in more secure possession of large parts of the country than at any previous time. Nor was it possible to persuade the Chinese Nationalist leader to any accommodation with the Communists. Negotiations to this end were undertaken with the blessing of the Americans as early as 1944. They were fruitless, and it is highly unlikely that even if Chiang had been more flexible, the Communists themselves would have agreed to any terms that did not give them the prospect of ultimate control. To put the matter broadly, all the elements that led to the collapse of American policy in China were in evidence before the end of the war. The United States had associated itself with a regime which, though containing many honorable men, was incapable of unifying and governing the country. The fact that it has appeared to most Americans as preferable to the crude and violent dictatorship that exists on the mainland cannot blind us to these essential facts.

Roosevelt, like Wilson twenty-five years before, cherished the idea of an association of nations for the maintenance of peace. The matter was discussed by Secretary Hull at Moscow in the fall of 1943, and Stalin's support secured. It was the subject of long deliberations at the famous Dumbarton Oaks conferences in the summer of 1944; the President issued a call for a conference to meet at San Francisco in the month of April, 1945. Just as the conference was assembling, Franklin D. Roosevelt was fatally stricken at Warm Springs, where he had gone for a few days' vacation. But he had paved the way, at least, for its success at home. A powerful bipartisan delegation represented the United States, and the United

Nations Charter drawn there was to be ratified in the Senate by the amazing vote of 82 to 2.

It is no part of our purpose to pursue the story of American diplomacy further; but relevant to the narrative is some comment on the view that was circulated after the war, for example, by such an eminent historian as Charles A. Beard, that American entry into the world conflict was an egregious mistake. It is true that when the peril from Hitler and from militarist Japan was exorcised, a new and terrible danger appeared in the form of Russian Communist imperialism, a danger still confronting America. But to say on this account that the whole policy was in error is to underestimate the possible consequences of the opposite course of action. What if a psychopathic tyrant like Hitler controlled Europe at the end of the war? What kind of world would it have been had such a man been in possession of the weapons of destruction that are available today? What kind of world would it have been if Germany and a Hitlerian Russia had joined hands once again, as they did in 1939? We have, of course, no certain answer to these questions, but they ought to induce reflection and lead us to abstain from dogmatism which brands the American part in the war as futile. In the Orient, it is true, we have seen a new tyranny replace the militarism of Japan. But the Japanese conquest at its height embraced Burma, Indonesia, the Philippines, the islands of the Pacific, and threatened Australia and New Zealand. Was it useless to beat back this threat in the East? Not many think so. The truth of the matter is that we err, and always will err, if we think of war as a universal solvent. War creates as well as solves problems. Life is a succession of challenges. We should take great pride in having met the challenge of 1941–45 and be heartened by the experience of those years to face the challenges of the future.

Arms and Diplomacy

The foreign affairs of the Roosevelt administration were among the most fateful in the history of the republic. Just as the New Deal needs analysis in an objective spirit, so, too, the foreign policy of the period calls for a retrospective judgment.

First, what of the role of the President? In the first six years of his terms of office Roosevelt was preoccupied with domestic problems. The great achievement in the field of foreign affairs was in the consolidation of the good-neighbor policy. But it must be confessed that this contribution stands alone. There may have been good reasons to torpedo the London Economic Conference, but the President's action was hardly conducive to better understanding between the United States and Europe. In the isolationist years, the years of the neutrality acts, the President seems in the main to have gone with the tide. There is certainly nothing very inspiring about the American attitude in the Italian-Ethiopian problem and little to praise of policy toward Europe in general. The inaction of this period is most fairly judged if it is placed alongside the fatuous policy of Britain and France in permitting Hitler to strengthen himself more and more and if it is regarded as an accurate expression of the mood of the time. And it should be remembered, on the other side of the account, that the President sought to arouse the nation from its lethargy as early as October, 1937, in the famous "quarantine" speech in Chicago, and that he lent his influence to the expansion of the navy long before the international events of 1939 and 1940.

By 1939 Roosevelt clearly discerned the peril from the totalitarian regimes, especially the peril from Hitler. It is impossible not so to credit him unless one takes the extreme and, for most of us, the unacceptable view that there *was* no peril and that no action of

165

any kind save preparation for our own defense was required. Once we accept the view that the interests and safety of the United States were in jeopardy, we must recognize the President's foresight in facing this issue. The speech of January, 1939, already quoted, shows a depth of insight into the possibilities of modern war and into the scope of new weapons that entitles us to regard it as high statesmanship. Roosevelt's early espousal of the repeal of the arms embargo and his prompt action after the beginning of the war in calling Congress together to effect that repeal were an example of leadership. Even more his Charlottesville speech, after the fall of France, deserves great praise, especially because it came in an election year.

He took the initiative in the enactment of lend-lease in 1941, and he made the necessary decisions to see that the lend-lease cargoes were protected. Just when he made up his mind to speed the tempo of American action, we cannot say; but by September, 1941, he acted in a way that suggested that he regarded full participation in the struggle as essential. He challenged Germany directly on the seas, and informal warfare against the submarine followed. Was he seeking by this time to commit the nation fully? We do not know. If he *did* wish full participation, could he have led the nation into war on land and sea alike had it not been for the Japanese attack on Pearl Harbor? It is by no means certain.

Roosevelt did not always lead. He often waited upon public opinion before acting, as in the case of the bases-destroyer deal and in the adoption of conscription. He equivocated miserably in the campaign of 1940. He was by no means completely ingenuous in his handling of the naval-escort question immediately after the adoption of lend-lease. He was obviously concerned, perhaps unduly concerned, with the strength of the America Firsters. Even when he decided upon more vigorous action in September, 1941, he was either uncandid or ill-informed. For, in the case of the "Greer," the naval vessel attacked at that time, he described it as "a peaceful vessel carrying the mails to Iceland," whereas it was really reporting to British planes the position of a German submarine.

His policy with regard to Japan is more difficult to analyze. Let us repeat that it is pure legend to suggest that he worked to provoke the attack on Pearl Harbor. In the main, it is right to say that he was cautious in opposing the Japanese advance and that he had no desire to precipitate a struggle in the Orient. But he would not yield to any question of principle; especially he would not abandon China. Some people believe, as we have seen, that he missed a chance at understanding at the time of Prince Konoye's overtures. His decision to impose an embargo on trade, understandable and defensible as it was, in the upshot made conflict more likely.

If one looks at the broad picture for these middle years, it seems right to say that the President grasped the implications of the world struggle earlier and more perceptively than most and that in action he was sometimes bold, sometimes cautious, sometimes urged on by conviction of the peril, and sometimes heeding the siren voice of political opportunism. But the major emphasis must be, not on the limitations, but on the statesmanship of Roosevelt's course.

We now come to Roosevelt and the war itself. And here, as in viewing the New Deal, we must beware of an overpersonalized judgment. War is the ultimate example of collective action in a society. To concentrate on any individual in describing it is certainly a historical error. The capacity of generals, the bravery of soldiers in the field, the high and fruitful energy of industrialists, the devotion of labor, the loyalty of the individual citizen—all play a fundamental part in the outcome. To attribute victory to one man would be absurd.

Yet Roosevelt played a highly important part in the winning of the war. The politician was submerged in the war leader. Secretary of War Henry L. Stimson, who always approached judgment of the President with at least a partial detachment derived from his Republican faith, nevertheless paid tribute to the manner in which the President discharged his responsibilities and showed his indifference to political considerations of the meaner type. In the conduct of the struggle Roosevelt paid heed to the advice of his generals and military advisers, and, in only a single instance and that a minor one, did he reverse their decision. In one sense he reinforced them, for he lent the weight of his authority and prestige to their judgment. Moreover, *one* military decision could be made by him alone. How to balance the demands of the war against Japan with the demands of the war against Hitler was, in the nature of the case, a controversial matter and one on which a division of opinion naturally existed among the military themselves. In giving full weight to the war in Europe where the United States had allies and faced a far greater peril than the peril from Japan, the President performed an essential public service. Once that decision was taken, he backed up General Marshall and his military advisers in giving central significance to the great cross-Channel invasion project. There were errors in the conduct of the war as there always are in matters so complex. General Chiang Kai-shek's capacity for resistance was much overestimated. The real weakness of Japan in 1945 was not accurately evaluated in Washington. But in these matters the decisions were by no means those of the President alone.

What are we to think of Roosevelt's war diplomacy? The connection with Vichy France, the subject of much criticism at the time, undoubtedly facilitated the invasion of North Africa. The Spaniards were brought more and more into the balance against Germany. The weakness in the Rooseveltian diplomacy was faith in the good intentions of the Kremlin. He was overconfident of his personal capacity to deal shrewdly with the Russian dictator; he had, undoubtedly, an exaggerated faith in the possibility of getting on with the Communists at the end of the war. It is necessary to add that he shared this faith with what was probably a majority of the American people. Of those who had an opinion in the first months of 1945, in a remarkable public opinion poll, two of every three persons believed that it was possible to "do business" with Moscow. The speed of our demobilization in 1945 and 1946 is another evidence of the failure of American opinion to recognize the pattern that was forming after victory. Of Yalta we need to say no more than has been already said.

One last comment on the personal diplomacy of the President. It was Roosevelt who pressed for the Charter of the United Nations and who called the San Francisco conference which convened after his death. In seeking to substitute some other procedure for that of war in the settlement of international disputes, he was at one with the American people. A judgment of the utility of the UN as an instrument of peace must be a balanced one. Some dangerous controversies have been settled by it; but the existence of the cold war and the system of alliances built up since 1945 do not inspire complete confidence in the machinery of the Charter. On the other hand, the UN has been useful as a means of encouraging technical advance, of dealing with the problems of disease, of bringing together representatives of many nations for the discussion of public questions, of educating many people to the realities of international politics. There are few persons who, whatever their criticism of its weaknesses, would wish to dispense with it.

We must now look at the war from a broader point of view than that of the personality of the President. What does it suggest as to the character of the American people? What were its results? We have already commented on the sense of social discipline that the

The New Age of Franklin Roosevelt, 1932–45

Americans displayed during the period of the conflict and on the truly formidable energies that the struggle unleashed. After 1945 no one could doubt that, however slow to anger they might be, the citizens of the United States would be the most dangerous of foes once their passions were aroused. No one could deny the range of their organizing abilities or their tenacity in the pursuit of their goal. Yet, true as this certainly was, it was also true that even in 1945, after crushing a dangerous and impacable foe, Americans were still naïve with regard to the role of power in international affairs. The speedy demobilization of 1945 and 1946 attested all too clearly that they failed to recognize force as the authority behind influential voices in the international forum. Only the harsh and aggressive policies of their former ally, the Soviet Union, convinced them that they had to be armed to sustain their interests and ideals. They, like their wartime leader, dodged this truth in 1945.

Despite the grim fact that more than 150,000 Americans were killed and four times that number wounded in the war, certain social gains resulted from the mass effort. One of these, the by-product of modern warfare, was an advance in medical science. A sensational forward movement in the use of penicillin led to the cure of a whole range of diseases. A tremendous campaign against malaria was made possible by the new insecticide known as DDT. Blood plasma became a fundamental aid in curing serious injuries.

The war was to have a great impact in the field of education. During the struggle Congress had passed the great statute known as the "G.I. Bill of Rights," by which educational opportunities at an advanced level were offered to veterans. The measure gave a substantial impetus to the growth of the universities. It was one factor, by no means the only one, which underlined the increasing tendency in the United States to broaden the field of academic life and which gave to American institutions of higher learning a special flavor. In Europe, even today, the university is a gateway to a professional career; in America, more and more, it has become something very different, with a wide range of "vocational" subjects and with an array of courses that would make a European gasp. It has, by the sweep of its appeal, provided an unrivaled instrument of social fluidity and given to many persons not destined for the professions a broader and more liberal view of life.

One of the most important social results of the war was the impetus given to population growth. In the Depression period the birth rate had sharply declined. It climbed again in the forties and was to remain at a high level thereafter. The early marriages of the war years and the G.I. Bill of Rights, with its inducements to married veterans, contributed to this result. In the long run, the change in this regard must be thought of as contributing a vital element to the economic and social strength of the nation.

In the economic field, the entry of the United States into the world conflict did what the Roosevelt administration had been unable to do. The scourge of unemployment, still serious in 1938, was eliminated. By the end of 1939, a year of expanding aid to the Allies and of rearmament, it had dropped to about five and one-half million. By 1944 it was only 670,000. Unsavory as it may be to recognize the fact that government spending on a colossal scale had accomplished the virtual extinction of this serious problem, there could be no doubt that this was precisely the case. It is not necessary to argue that this was the only way the problem could have been solved or that it is the only way out of a future depression—if one comes. But it is necessary to face the fact that it had been eliminated in this fashion.

In a sense, the economic pattern fixed in the years of the New Deal was consolidated by the events of 1941–45. It would have been impossible to break the power of organized labor in American life at the end of the war, and, in truth, there was no attempt to do so. Curbs there were to be, on what some men deemed the excessive power of the unions, but a reversion to the practices of 1932 or 1933 was generally recognized to be out of the question. In the same way, the expansion of American agriculture, made necessary during the struggle, tended to fix more firmly in the American economy the principle of subsidy to the growers of the great staples. To have left the farmer to readjust himself without government aid was something no administration and no Congress could have possibly done.

The great positive change on the economic side was in the increased confidence felt by the business classes, as a result of their immense achievements and high profits during the war years. In a very real sense, the war may be said to have raised the morale of the entrepreneurs and to have underlined their contribution to society. It would have been impossible by 1945 to engage in the melancholy predictions with regard to American capitalism that were so common in the Depression.

On the political front, the war had less far-reaching effects. It did not produce immediately, as had the war of 1917–18, a sharp reaction against the party in power. Yet by 1946 the Republicans had captured the Congress, and they were to come nearer to taking the Presidency in 1948 than they had in many years.

In the international scene, however, the changes were more significant. Though there were no doubt Americans who wished to withdraw from the world stage, the world situation in 1945 made this impossible. For good or for evil, the United States had a great role to play, a role which it could not avoid. And this fact was to become clearer and clearer. One of its consequences was a tendency toward a broader view of foreign policy than had existed in the past, and that was manifested in the growth of the spirit of bipartisan collaboration. This is not to say that the partisan spirit was eliminated, for there is no indication today that this is possible. But the UN Charter was approved with virtual unanimity (a striking contrast with the battle over the League in 1919 and 1920). The Marshall plan (1947) and the North Atlantic treaty (1949) were warmly supported by both parties. Though the less scrupulous politicians continued to indulge in misrepresentation and to discharge their usual venom, there were many instances of united action in the foreign field. The country, so knit together in the war period, faced many of the issues of the postwar years with substantial solidarity.

There is a final point to be made. Though the atom bomb, which terminated the war against Japan, was not detonated until after the President's death, the researches which made it possible were carried on, as we have seen, with his encouragement during the period of the war. These researches, we now know, were only the beginning of a process so portentous that it staggers the mind and baffles the imagination. The war of 1945, in this sense, opens a new era in the history of mankind. What does this era portend? Will man find in the new achievements of science the way to peace and plenty? Will he recognize that to unleash the passions of international conflict on a grand scale may well lead to mutual destruction? Or will he come to believe that war is now outmoded and turn his energies to the use of the new forces of science for the peace and progress of mankind? These are the fateful questions we have to face today.

Important Dates

1933   The "Hundred Days," March 9–June 16
       Agricultural Adjustment Act, May 12
       Tennessee Valley Authority Act, May 18
       Glass-Steagall Banking Reform Act, June 16
       National Industrial Recovery Act, June 16
       Public Works Administration established, June 16

1934   Securities and Exchange Commission authorized, June 6
       American Liberty League formed (reaction against the administration), August 23
       Democratic congressional majorities increased in the election, November 6

1935   President's message swings left, January 4
       Works Progress Administration created, April 8
       N.I.R.A. invalidated by Supreme Court, May 27
       National Labor Relations Act, July 5
       Public Utilities Holding Company Act, August 26
       Revenue Act of 1935 ("share the wealth"), August 30

1936   A.A.A. invalidated by Supreme Court, January 6
       Roosevelt overwhelmingly re-elected, November 3

1937   President announces court-packing plan, February 5
       Supreme Court reverses itself on minimum wage, March 29
       Wagner Act declared constitutional by Supreme Court, April 12

Important Dates

Social Security Act declared constitutional by Supreme Court, May 24

President's "quarantine" speech at Chicago hints departure from isolationism, October 5

1938 New A.A.A., February 16
Fair Labor Standards Act, June 25

1939 President warns of danger from abroad, January 4
World War II breaks out in Europe, September 2
Arms embargo repealed, November 4

1940 With fall of France imminent, President in Charlottesville speech pledges aid to the democracies, June 10
Destroyers-bases deal, September 2
President re-elected (over Willkie) for third term, November 5

1941 Lend-lease enacted, March 12
Hitler invades Russia, June 22
United States severs commerial relations with Japan as result of Japanese occupation of southern Indo-China, July 24
President orders navy to attack U-boats on sight, September 12
Pearl Harbor bombed by Japanese, December 7

1942 Japanese decisively checked at Midway, June 5–7
Guadalcanal occupation inaugurates United States offensive in the Pacific, August 7
North Africa invaded by Allied forces, November 8

1943 Mussolini falls, July 25
Italy invaded by Allies, September 3
Roosevelt, Churchill, and Stalin confer at Teheran, November 28–December 1

1944 D-Day (Allies invade Normandy), June 6
Japanese fleet decisively defeated in Leyte Gulf, June 18–19

1945 Yalta Conference, February 3–11
Roosevelt dies; Truman becomes President, April 12
V-E Day (Germany surrenders), May 7
V-J Day (surrender of Japan ends the war), September 2

Suggested Reading

The literature on the New Deal and on World War II is vast. This brief bibliography comprises a list of books of interest to the general reader and yet making an important contribution to the history of the period.

For the personality of Roosevelt one of the most perceptive studies is that of Frances Perkins, *The Roosevelt I Knew* (1946). Miss Perkins was associated with the President closely from 1929 until his death. Her book deals mostly with his attitude toward domestic problems and with the development of his personality. It is not uncritical. Another study by a close associate is Samuel Rosenman's *Working with Roosevelt* (1952). This work sheds particular light on Roosevelt as a tactician and political leader. No President other than F. D. R. had a wife who took such a keen, intelligent, and humane interest in politics. It is impossible to dispense with *This I Remember* by Eleanor Roosevelt (1949). Finally, in this category must be placed John Gunther's analysis, *Roosevelt in Retrospect* (1950). The tone of this book is journalistic, but the general approach is highly laudatory. There are many insights and not a few penetrating criticisms. If one wants to read a book which castigates Roosevelt, unfairly and bitterly, but which offsets the

Suggested Reading

large literature in praise of him, one should look at John T. Flynn's *The Roosevelt Myth* (1948).

For broader studies of the period an anticipatory note should first be made of Frank Freidel's monumental biography, *Franklin D. Roosevelt* (3 vols., 1952–56), which is expected to run to seven volumes but which has in 1956 merely reached the period of the governorship, and Arthur Schlesinger, Jr.'s *Age of Roosevelt*, which will run to three. The best political study of the years down to 1940, and of Roosevelt's central role in them, is James M. Burns's *The Lion and the Fox* (1956). Burns is particularly interested in the tactical aspects of the Roosevelt career; his book is lively, with a vivid sense of personality and with many interesting insights. Basil Rauch has written two general works, one a *History of the New Deal* (1944) and another *Roosevelt from Munich to Pearl Harbor* (1950). Rauch's first book is a useful summary; his second, though somewhat argumentative, is an interesting analysis of the Roosevelt foreign policy. For a more critical view one should read Edgar E. Robinson's *The Roosevelt Leadership, 1933–45* (1955). Professor Robinson tries hard to be objective, but his devotion to former President Hoover and his natural conservatism make this a difficult task. He does not satisfactorily explain the enormous pull of Roosevelt's personality. He is, however, a useful antidote to the standard accounts of the New Deal and of Roosevelt's foreign policy.

There are some very important books by Roosevelt's advisers. *The Memoirs of Cordell Hull* (2 vols., 1948) are, of course, particularly interesting in the field of foreign policy. They are filled with self-praise, and they exaggerate the Secretary's role; but they provide a broad view of the diplomatic scene, of Roosevelt's cavalier methods with his advisers, and of the difficulties the administration sometimes faced in Congress. There can be no doubt of their fundamental value. Obviously, one of the most interesting of the Roosevelt cabinet was Harold Ickes. His *The Autobiography of a Curmudgeon* (1943) and his *The Secret Diary of Harold L. Ickes* (3 vols., 1953–54), though filled with trivia and reflecting his personal likes and dislikes, add much flavor to the period. Another narrative of primary interest is Robert Sherwood's *Roosevelt and Hopkins* (1948). Here was one of the most intimate friendships of the period, though clouded at the end of the President's career. Both for the domestic problem of relief and still more for the problems of foreign policy, this book is essential reading, candid, well-balanced, and penetrating. A most interesting insight into the President's policies, especially for the earlier years, is provided by Raymond Moley's *After Seven Years* (1939). Moley was gradually estranged from Roosevelt and moved more and more into the conservative camp. But he gives us an excellent picture of the period 1933–35, and his critical judgments are of great value in attaining a sound perspective. For political maneuver, one should look at James A. Farley's *Behind the Ballots* (1938). Here a master mechanician throws much light on political methods. For a longer and critical view, it is worthwhile to read *Jim Farley's Story: The Roosevelt Years* (1948).

On special aspects of the New Deal the following are particularly useful. For the passage of the Wagner Act the key work is that of Irving Bernstein, *The New Deal Collective Bargaining Policy* (1950). Bernstein made a fundamental contribution in this book in showing how very cagey was the President's attitude toward the labor problem. For the division in the labor movement Herbert Harris' *Labor's Civil War* (1940) is illuminating, and for a general history of labor, written with his useful discrimination in the selection of his facts, one should read Foster Rhea Dulles, *Labor in America* (1949).

Suggested Reading

For the monetary policy of the New Deal G. G. Johnson, Jr.'s *The Treasury and Monetary Policy, 1933–38* (1939) is the best special study. "The Morgenthau Diaries" in *Collier's* (September 27–November 1, 1947) make a fundamental contribution in this field and shed much light on Roosevelt's personality. For the WPA, besides Sherwood, one should read Arthur W. MacMahon *et al.*, *The Administration of Federal Work Relief* (1941), which is an objective analysis of a very important problem. For a scientific analysis of the role of WPA in stimulating the economy, J. K. Galbraith and G. G. Johnson, Jr.'s *Economic Effects of Federal Works Expenditures, 1933–1938* (1940) is useful. For the N.I.R.A. the most colorful narrative, though hardly the most detached, is that of Hugh Johnson, *The Blue Eagle from Egg to Earth* (1935). For a judgment on the act, it is worthwhile to consult the "Report of the President's Committee of Analysis" (75th Cong., 1st sess.; H.R. Doc. 158). On the agricultural problem a valuable and highly objective brief account is that of Professor Murray R. Benedict in his book, *Farm Policies of the United States* (1953).

On the struggle over the Supreme Court, every interested person should read Robert H. Jackson's *The Struggle for Judicial Supremacy* (1941). Jackson was at the time Solicitor-General; he was later to be one of the most distinguished of the Roosevelt appointees to the Court itself. He saw the controversy, therefore, from both points of view, and his assessment is an extremely penetrating one. One of the foremost scholars in this field is Professor E. S. Corwin of Princeton. His two books, *Constitutional Revolution, Ltd.* (1946) and *Court over Constitution* (1938), show how an eminent, rather conservative, and always independent thinker evaluated the judicial history of the New Deal period. A colorful journalistic account is Joseph Alsop and Turner Catledge's *The 168 Days* (1938). The point of view of Justice Hughes is best seen in the highly sympathetic biography of Merle J. Pusey, *Charles Evans Hughes* (2 vols., 1951).

For an understanding of the war period, D. M. Nelson's *Arsenal of Democracy* (1941) is required reading; it provides a striking picture of American industry's role in the struggle. The contribution of the scientists is set forth in James P. Baxter's *Scientists against Time* (1946), again a book for which there is no substitute as far as the layman is concerned. On the side of diplomatic history, there is quite a body of literature, some of it highly controversial. The scholarly masterpiece for the period is the two-volume work of William L. Langer and S. Everett Gleason, *The Challenge to Isolation, 1937–1940* (1952) and *The Undeclared War* (1953). Langer and Gleason had free access to government documents and have prepared an account that, while limited to the diplomatic events and their immediate background, is without a rival. Herbert Feis, who had large experience in the State Department, has written two highly important volumes, *The China Tangle* (1953), by far the best account of our relations with Chiang Kai-shek and calculated to destroy all illusion about that gentleman, and *The Road to Pearl Harbor* (1950), an excellent brief account of American diplomacy in relation to the Orient. For Japanese matters J. C. Grew's *Ten Years in Japan* (1944) is indispensable as the work of one of the most eminent of American career diplomats. There is material not to be found elsewhere, including a colorful account of visits to Hitler and to Mussolini, in Sumner Welles's *Time for Decision* (1944). Welles, as stated in the text, was the close friend of the President and was Under-Secretary of State at a critical period. If one wants a critical view of the Roosevelt diplomacy, one can find it in Charles A. Beard's two volumes, *American Foreign Policy in the Making, 1932–1940* (1946) and *President Roosevelt and the Coming of the War* (1948). The tone is strident is the second volume. From a similar view, a bit more objective but with moments of acidity, see Charles C. Tansill, *The Black Door to War* (1952).

For the military history Eisenhower's *Crusade in Europe* (1948) is a lively and candid narrative. It may be supplemented by Omar Bradley's *A Soldier's Story* (1951). Though written from the British point of view, the Churchill volumes on the war are not only of the first literary merit but add much to the knowledge of operations and to the general picture of the war. They are *The Gathering Storm* (1948), *Their Finest Hour* (1949), *The Grand Alliance* (1950), *The Hinge of Fate* (1950), *Closing the Ring* (1952), and *Triumph and Tragedy* (1954). On the naval side, Professor Samuel E. Morison has written a series of volumes, *History of United States Naval Operations in World War II* (14 vols., 1947——). Professor Morison has verve and literary style, and, despite the detail of these books, they are intensely interesting, especially the third volume on *The Rising Sun in the Pacific* (1948), which contains an excellent analysis of the events preceding Pearl Harbor and of the attack itself. E. J. King and W. M. Whitehill's *Fleet Admiral King* (1952) is a good summary and gives an insight into one of the great, and possibly less appreciated, figures of the war period. Curiously enough, General MacArthur has never written of his own exploits in detail, but the reader can find a rhapsodic account in Courtney Vhitney's *A Rendezvous with MacArthur* (1956), written under the General's eye. Somewhat more objective but still biased is Frazier Hunt's *The Untold Story of MacArthur* (1954). As a general work on the strategy of the war Fletcher Pratt's *War for the World* (1950) is valuable.

Index

Index

Index

Index

McCormick, Robert R., as promoter of America First, 115

McReynolds, J. C., as associate justice of Supreme Court, attitude toward New Deal legislation, 41, 43

Manchuria: attitude of F. D. R. toward situation, 89; occupation of, by Japanese (1931), 84

Marshall, General George C.: criticism of, for defeat at Pearl Harbor, 129, 130; names Eisenhower head of army, 147; opposes strong United States action in Orient, 123; supports plan to invade Europe, 168

Marshall plan (1947), economic aid to Europe, 173

Matsuoka, Yosuke: as foreign minister of Japan signs neutrality pact with Russia, 124; visits Rome, Berlin, and Moscow, 121

Medical science, advancement in, due to war, 170

Merchant ships, bill to arm, passed (1941), 121

Midway, Battle of (1942), 152

Miller-Tydings Act (1936), manufacturers permitted to fix minimum retail prices, 51

Millis, Walter, *The Road to War*, 95

Minimum wage laws, discussion of and decisions on, 48–49, 60, 67

Mobilization: industrial production, increase in, 134; success of, 131

Moley, Raymond: ghost writer for F. D. R., 16; at London Economic Conference, 93

Montgomery, General Bernard L., part in European campaign of World War II, 151–52

Morgenthau, Henry: as Secretary of Treasury supports F. D. R.'s financial policy, 21; speech on government deficit, 66; suggests plan for reduction of Germany's industrial power, 158

Morgenthau plan (Quebec, 1944) for reduction of Germany's industrial power, 158

Moscicki, President (Poland), letter to, from F. D. R. (1939), 107

Moscow conference (1943), plan for "unconditional surrender" pledged by Allies, 159

Munich pact (1938): attitude of Americans toward, 103; forced by Hitler, 104–5

Mussolini, Benito: attack on Ethiopia (1935), 98–100; collapse of regime (1943), 148; declares war on United States (1941), 129; invasion of Albania (1939), 106; joins Hitler as ally (1940), 109

Nagasaki, bombing of, significance of, 3

National Association of Manufacturers: campaign against NLB, 37, 38; opposition to F. D. R., 40

National Conference Board, figures on employment given, 51, 79

National Defense Research Committee (1940), in charge of development of the A-bomb, 140–43

National Guard, called out by F. D. R. for extensive training, 113

National income, increase in (1936), 51

National Industrial Recovery Act (1933): cited, 24, 25, 26, 27, 35, 38, 47, 51, 64, 72; declared unconstitutional by Supreme Court (1935), 38, 43; difficulties in enforcement of, 44; explanation of, 15; failure of, 75; similarity to trade association movement, 71

National Labor Board (1933): story of, 37–38; Supreme Court decision upholds power of, 61

National Labor Relations Board (1934): establishment of, 38, 39; opposition to, 39; powers of, 39

National Longshoremen's Board, settles strike, 37

189

Index

Index

THE CHICAGO HISTORY OF AMERICAN CIVILIZATION

Daniel J. Boorstin, Editor

Edmund S. Morgan, *The Birth of the Republic: 1763–89*

Marcus Cunliffe, *The Nation Takes Shape: 1789–1837*

John Hope Franklin, *Reconstruction: After the Civil War*

Samuel P. Hays, *The Response to Industrialism: 1885–1914*

William E. Leuchtenburg, *The Perils of Prosperity: 1914–32*

Dexter Perkins, *The New Age of Franklin Roosevelt: 1932–45*

Herbert Agar, *The Price of Power: America since 1945*

*   *   *

Robert H. Bremner, *American Philanthropy*

Richard M. Dorson, *American Folklore*

John Tracy Ellis, *American Catholicism*

Nathan Glazer, *American Judaism*

William T. Hagan, *American Indians*

Winthrop S. Hudson, *American Protestantism*

Maldwyn Allen Jones, *American Immigration*

Robert G. McCloskey, *The American Supreme Court*

Howard H. Peckham, *The War for Independence: A Military History*

*Howard H. Peckham, *The Colonial Wars: 1689–1762*

Henry Pelling, *American Labor*

Charles P. Roland, *The Confederacy*

Otis A. Singletary, *The Mexican War*

John F. Stover, *American Railroads*

*Bernard A. Weisberger, *The American Newspaperman*

* Available in cloth only. All other books published in both cloth and paperback editions.

DATE DUE			
APR 7 '65			
MAY 28 '65			
NOV 2 '66			
JAN 17 '67			
JAN 31 '67			
APR 18 '67			
MAY 2 '67			
DEC 11 '68			
7/9/73			
JAN 28 '75			
MAY 14 '84			
MAR 23			
DEC 14 '93			
MAR 2 0 1998			
GAYLORD			PRINTED IN U.S.A.